Daily Discoveries for April

Thematic Learning Activities for *EVERY DAY*

Written by Elizabeth Cole Midgley

Illustrated by Jennette Guymon-King

Teaching & Learning Company

1204 Buchanan St., P.O. Box 10

Carthage, IL 62321-0010

This book belongs to

____

⚠

Several of the activities in this book involve preparing, tasting and sharing food items. We urge you to be aware of any food allergies or restrictions your students may have and to supervise these activities diligently. All food-related suggestions are identified with this allergy-alert symbol: ⚠

Please note: small food items (candies, raisins, cereal, etc.) can also pose a choking hazard.

Cover art by Jennette Guymon-King

ISBN No. 1-57310-469-8

Printing No. 987654321

Teaching & Learning Company
1204 Buchanan St., P.O. Box 10
Carthage, IL 62321-0010

Table of Contents

Dear Teacher or Parent,

Due to the stimulus of a high-tech world, parents and teachers are often faced with the challenge of how to capture the attention of a child and create an atmosphere of meaningful learning opportunities. Often we search for new ways to meet this challenge and help young people transfer their knowledge, skills and experiences from one area to another. Subjects taught in isolation can leave a feeling of fragmentation. More and more educators are looking for ways to be able to integrate curriculum so that their students can fully understand how things relate to each other.

The Daily Discoveries series has been developed to that end. The premise behind this series has been, in part, the author's educational philosophy: anything can be taught and absorbed by others in a meaningful way, depending upon its presentation.

In this series, each day has been researched around the history of a specific individual or event and has been developed into a celebration or theme with integrated curriculum areas. In this approach to learning students draw from their own experience and understanding of things, to a level of processing new information and skills.

The Daily Discoveries series is an almanac-of-sorts, 12 books (one for each month) that present a thematically based curriculum for grades K-6. The series contains hundreds and hundreds of resources and ideas that can be a natural springboard to learning. These ideas have been used in the classroom and at home, and are fun as well as educationally sound. The activities have been endorsed by professors, teachers, parents and, best of all, by children.

The Daily Discoveries series can be used in the following ways for school or home:

- to develop new skills and reinforce previous learning
- to create a sense of fun and celebration every day
- as tutoring resources
- as enrichment activities that can be used as time allows
- for family fun activities

Sincerely,

Elizabeth

Elizabeth Cole Midgley

April Fools' Day

April 1

Setting the Stage

- Write on the board, "Only two more days of school! . . . . April Fools!"

- Before school, write everyone's name backwards (Fred is Derf) and try to call them (and yourself) by backwards names for the rest of the day. You may prefer to let students make up names for themselves today. Let students sign their papers all day with their backwards or made-up names.

- Throughout the day, do silly and unexpected things (wear sunglasses in the classroom, wear your clothes backwards, wear your socks over your shoes, etc.). Your students will never forget it!

- Display student work with a picture of a court jester and the caption: "No FOOLING, this is great work!"

- Construct a semantic web with words your students think of when you say, "April Fools' Day."

Historical Background

The first day of April is traditionally April Fools' Day. The celebration originated in France. On their new year's celebration, the first day of spring, the French exchange gifts and treats. When the calendar was changed in the 16th century, these practices were stopped except for those far out in the country who hadn't heard about the change. When some people continued to give gifts though the official celebration had ended, they were made fun of, called "fools" and became the object of practical jokes. As time went on and everyone finally heard about the change, people continued with the practical jokes just for fun!

Literary Exploration

Amelia Bedelia (series) by Peggy Parish
April Fools by Fernando Krahn
Diane Goode's Book of Silly Stories and Songs by Diane Goode
The Great School Lunch Rebellion by David Greenberg
It's April Fools Day! by Steven Kroll
Look Out, It's April Fool's Day by Frank Modell
The Laugh Book by JoAnna Cole and Stephanie Calmenson
Pictures to Stretch the Imagination by Mitsumasa Anno
The Random House Book of Humor for Children by Pamela Pollack
The Silliest Joke Book Ever by Victoria Hartman

April Fools' Day

April Fools' Day

Language Experience

- Explain how homonyms such as *know* and *no* or other figures of speech can "fool" us. Read aloud *The King Who Rained* or *A Chocolate Moose for Dinner* by Fred Gwynne. Challenge students to come up with other expressions that "fool" us.

- Let students suggest words that have the "oo" sound as in *fools.*

Writing Experience

- Encourage students to write about the funniest experience they ever had or the funniest April Fools joke they've heard of. See reproducible on page 11.

Math Experience

- Have some mixed-up math! Give students math problems with the answers (some right and some wrong). Students spot check and correct the ones that are wrong.

2 + 2 = 7

Science/Health Experience

- Some studies show that laughter improves a person's emotional health. Discuss how this might work.

Music/Dramatic Experience

- Let each student perform a comedy routine or tell a joke or riddle for the rest of the class.

Physical/Sensory Experience

- Play the Human Laugh game. Students lie on the floor with each person's head on another's stomach, linked together. The first person laughs hard and creates a "chain" of giggles that ripples down the line.

Physical/Sensory Experience continued

- Play You Can't Make Me Laugh. Students pair up and face each other, one with a serious face. The other one tries to make him or her laugh. When the serious one laughs, they switch roles. You may want to eliminate people from the game as they laugh and see who can stay serious the longest!

Arts/Crafts Experience

- Let each student create a "What's Wrong with This Page?" art picture. They can draw things that do not make sense or that are out of place such as glasses on a rabbit, a tail on a man, etc. Students exchange papers and circle or color the "wrong" things. See reproducible on page 12.

April Fools' Day
April Fools' Day

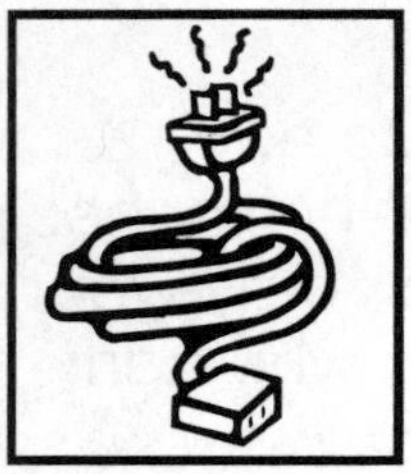

Extension Activities

- Have students create an acrostic poem. Write the words *April Fools* down the left-hand side of a piece of paper. Each line of the poem will begin with the corresponding letter. (Rhyming is optional.)

  April begins with a joke and a laugh
  Pranks, surprises, tricks and giggles
  Random acts of silliness abound

⚠ Since it's such a silly day and a time for laughter, serve miniature "Snickers™" candy bars!

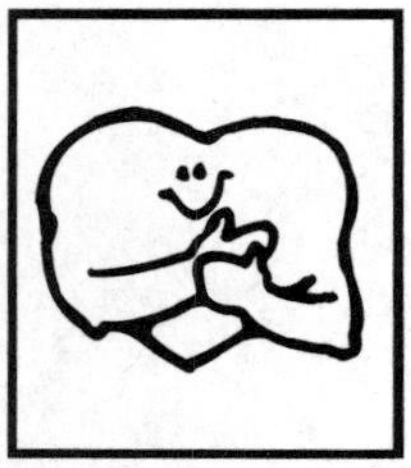

Values Education Experience

- Discuss the difference between harmless and harmful pranks on April Fools' Day.

Follow-Up/Homework Idea

- Challenge students to read a book backwards tonight!

Name: ______________________________

What's wrong with this page?

Storytelling Day

April 2

Setting the Stage

- Invite your students to dress up as their favorite storybook characters today.

- Display storybooks (such as those by Hans Christian Andersen) to capture your students' attention and get them excited about the day.
- Remind everyone to be sure and raise their "Hans" all day when asking or answering questions.
- Construct a semantic web with words your students think of when you say the word *storytelling*.

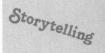

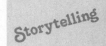

Historical Background

Author and storyteller Hans Christian Andersen was born in Odense, Denmark, on this day in 1805. Many of his fairy tales are classics of children's literature. He died in 1875.

Literary Exploration

The Emperor's New Clothes by Hans Christian Andersen
The Fairy Tale Life of Hans Christian Andersen by Eva Moore
The Fir Tree by Hans Christian Andersen
Hans Clodhopper by Hans Christian Andersen
It's Perfectly True by Janet Stevens
The Little Mermaid by Hans Christian Andersen
The Nightingale by Hans Christian Andersen
The Princess and the Pea by Hans Christian Andersen
Seven Stories by Hans Christian Andersen by Eric Carle
The Snow Queen by Hans Christian Andersen
Steadfast Tin Soldier by Hans Christian Andersen
The Stories of Hans Christian Andersen by Robert Mathias
Thumbelina by Hans Christian Andersen
The Ugly Duckling by Hans Christian Andersen
The Ugly Duckling by Daniel Sans Souchi

Language Experience

- Invite students who dressed up as storybook characters to share some clues about who they are or pantomime parts of their story. Other students can guess who they are.

- Have students tell their favorite fairy tales in their own words to the class. Encourage them to be dramatic and enthusiastic.

Writing Experience

- Challenge students to write stories for storytelling later in the day. Encourage them to include some of the things Andersen said are essential elements of a story: tragedy, comedy, irony and humor. Most of his stories also contained a of moral in the end. See pattern on page 18.

- Let students write about their favorite storybook characters and explain the reason for their choices.

Math Experience

- Have students survey other students around the school about their favorite storybook tales. Add the information to a class bar graph.

Social Studies Experience

- Study the life of Hans Christian Andersen.

- Have students locate Denmark on a world map or globe. What continent is it on?

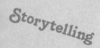

Music/Dramatic Experience

- Divide students into drama teams and let them act or present puppet shows of Andersen's fairy tales or other favorite stories. See reproducibles for Goldilocks and the Three Bears sack puppets on pages 19-22.

- Suggest a story topic (such as the 24-Hour Hero or The Girl Who Could Fly). Have one student start to tell the story, then another one take over with each student adding to the story.

Physical/Sensory Experience

- Students can take part in creative movement, waddling like a duck, dancing like a ballerina or marching like a tin soldier in Andersen's stories. Play music of various kinds and let students make up their dances as they go!

Arts/Crafts Experience

- Students will enjoy individually illustrating their favorite Hans Christian Andersen stories on art paper or working together on a class mural.
- Let students make giant storybooks! They can work in groups, each group member writing or illustrating a different part of the story. Then they put the pages in sequence and staple or tie them together for a big book.

Extension Activities

- Host a Storytelling Festival or Reader's Theater! Invite other adults (such as the school principal, nurse, custodian, secretary, parents and older students) to come and tell or read their favorite stories. (If you team teach with other teachers, have alternating storytelling festivities in each room and have students rotate from room to room.)

⚠ After reading *The Princess and the Pea* to your students, serve Princess and the Pea Cookies to students. Spread a white frosting "blanket" on a rectangular wafer cookie "bed." Students place a candy pea (from a specialty candy store) in the cookie. Then let students lay a piece of candy (such as a Sour Patch Kids™ candy girl) on the "bed."

⚠ Serve Danish pastries in honor of Hans Christian Andersen, the Danish author!

Follow-Up/Homework Idea

- Encourage students to check out one of Andersen's books from the library to read at home.

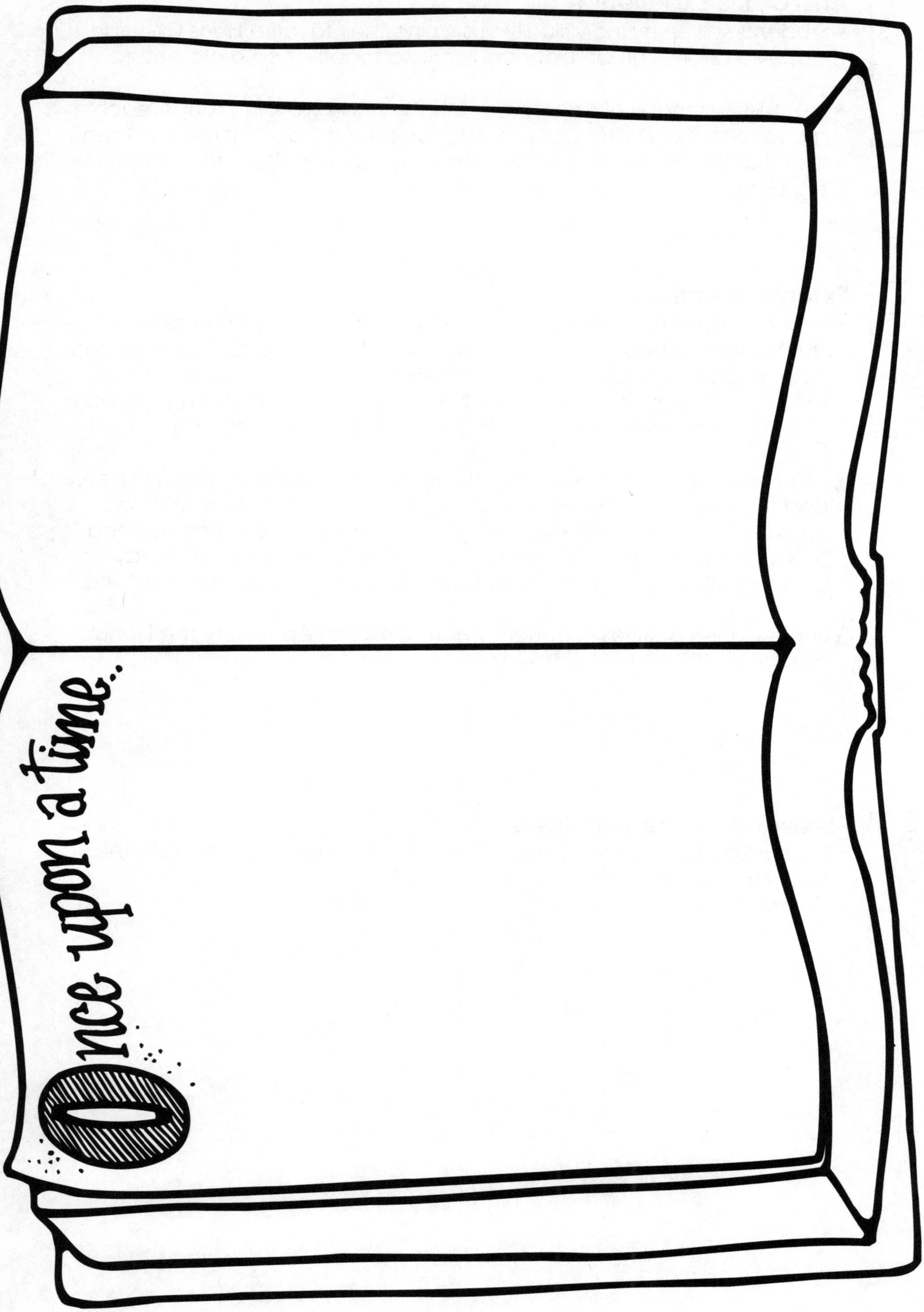
Once upon a time...

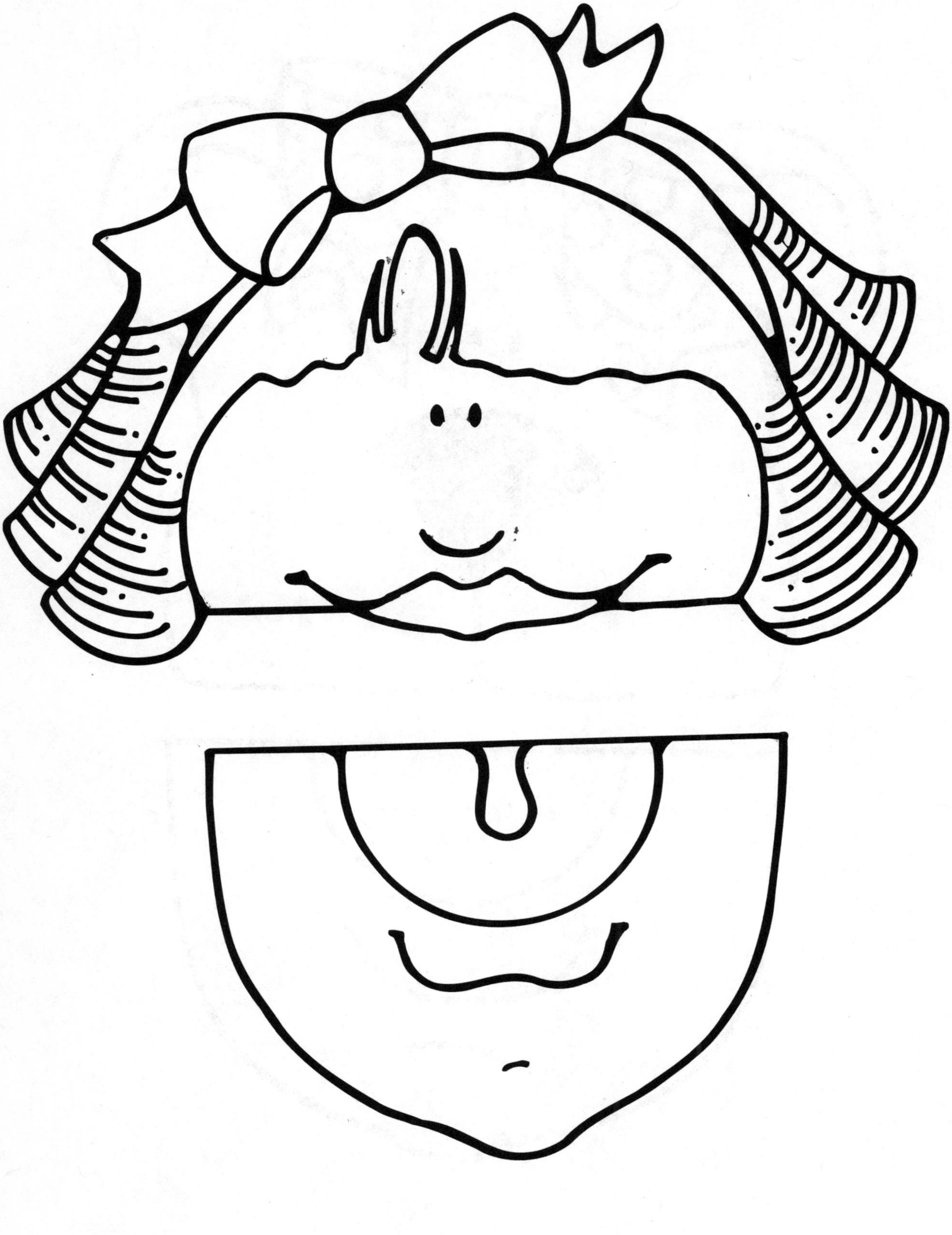

Under the Big Top Day

April 3

Setting the Stage

- Wear a clown costume to greet your students! Hang balloons everywhere. Borrow a colorful parachute from the P.E. Department to hang from the ceiling for a circus tent atmosphere.

- Construct a semantic map or web with facts your students know (or would like to know) about the circus.

Historical Background

The very first circus in the United States opened on this day in Philadelphia in 1793. It featured acrobatics, tricks on horseback, clowning and a tightrope walker. President George Washington was said to have attended one of the circus performances. By the 1800s circus animals and their trainers were a part of the show. Train transportation made circuses available in more and more cities across the United States. They became the most popular form of entertainment (until radio, movies and television). Many people still enjoy the circus. More than 40 circuses travel from town to town across America.

Literary Exploration

Bear Circus by W.P. Du Bois
Beastly Circus by Peggy Parish
Big Top Circus by Neil Johnson
Blue Bug's Circus by Virginia Poulet and Mary Maloney-Fleming
Brian Wildsmith's Circus by Brian Wildsmith
C Is for Circus by Bernice Chardiet
Circus by Dick Bruna
Circus by Beatrice DeRegniers
Circus by Lois Ehlert
The Circus by Heidi Goennel
Circus! by Mattie Lou O'Kelley
Circus by Jack Prelutsky
Circus Animals by Dianne Cassidy
Circus! Circus!: Poems by Lee Bennett Hopkins
Circus Girl by Michael Garland
The Circus in the Mist by Bruno Munari
Circus Numbers by Rodney Peppe
Circus People by Dianne Cassidy
Clowning Around: Jokes About the Circus by Rick and Ann Walton
Dr. Anno's Magical Midnight Circus by Mitsumasa Anno
Harriet Goes to the Circus by Betsy Maestro
How to Be a Clown by C.R. Meyer
If I Ran the Circus by Dr. Seuss
Inside the Circus by Frank Fitzgerald
Lottie's Circus by Joan W. Blos
Mirette on the Highwire by Emily Arnold McCully
Paper Circus: How to Create Your Own Circus by Robin West
Peter Spier's Circus by Peter Spier
See the Circus by H.A. Rey
Ten Little Circus Mice by Bob Beeson
The Toy Circus by Jan Wahl
Up Goes the Big Top by Bernard Garbutt

Language Experience

- Encourage your students in critical thinking with a Venn diagram showing the similarities and differences between a circus and a carnival.
- Circuses are usually advertised with "big" adjectives such as *collassal* or *stupendous.* Challenge students to think of other "big" adjectives.

Writing Experience

- Have each student submit in writing a proposal for a circus act or death-defying feat he or she would like to be involved in (clown, acrobat, lion tamer, juggler, snake charmer, mime, strong man, etc.).
- Give each student an animal cracker and have him or her write about that animal's act in the circus.
- See reproducible on page 30.

Math Experience

⚠ Have a guessing contest with a jar of jelly beans or peanuts. Let students estimate the number in the jar. Then count them together to see whose estimate was the closest. Eat a few, too!

- Read *Circus Numbers* by Rodney Peppe. Encourage students to make their own version of circus math books for young students.

Social Studies Experience

- Study ancient Rome's history of circular entertainment (gladiators and chariot races). The word *circus* comes from a latin word meaning, "circle."

- Let students research clown colleges. What do they teach? What are their students expected to do before graduating?

Music/Dramatic Experience

- Ask your school band to march around the school and play some marching tunes!

- Check out tapes or CDs of circus music at your local library: Copland's *Circus Music,* Schuman's *Carnival,* K.L. King's *Barnum and Bailey's Favorite,* Cleo Lane's *Send in the Clowns* or Saint Saens' *Carnival of the Animals.*

- Let each of your students "audition" to be a clown. Provide some props and funny clothing for those who want to look the part.

- Some students may want to "audition" for being the ringmaster who introduces each act. Let them tell some jokes from the book, *Clowning Around: Jokes About the Circus* by Rick Walton.

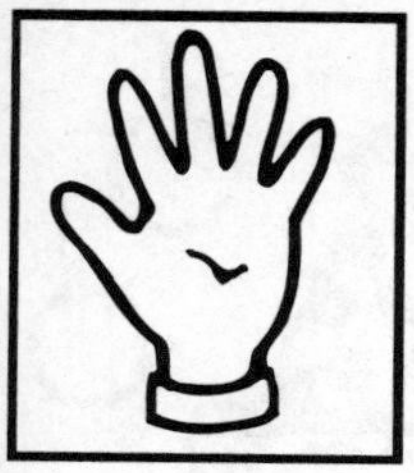

Physical/Sensory Experience

- Circus activities provide an opportunity for improving gross motor skills. Let your students walk the "tightrope" (a balance beam or a long piece of tape across the floor) for coordination, catch a beach ball, jump, tumble and march.

- Blindfold students one at a time and play Pin the Nose on the Clown (like Pin the Tail on the Donkey)! See patterns on page 31.

- Have a peanut race! Each students must race to the finish line holding a shelled peanut between the knees.
- Hold a Penny Pitching Contest! Pitch pennies into designated areas or jars. Award prizes to the best penny pitcher.

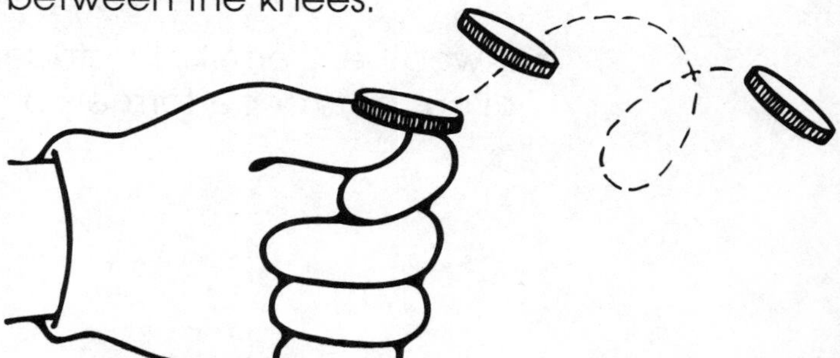

Physical/Sensory Experience continued

- Ask someone to be a good sport and let students toss wet sponges at him or her. The "target" can stick his or her head in an innertube for a frame.
- Let students try to juggle foam balls.

Arts/Crafts Experience

- Let students make their own circus animals (ponies, elephants or lions) from boxes and construction paper. The boxes should be big enough for the student to step into to make the animal "come alive."

- Students can draw large figures of a clown or circus performer with the face cut out. Hang the figures up and let students stand behind them and put their heads in the holes for instant camera photos. Let them take their photos home to show their families.
- If weather permits, let students make chalk drawings of their favorite circus acts or performers on the school sidewalk.

Arts/Crafts Experience

- Students love face painting as artists or recipients. Watercolors are easy to use and wash off easily. Or use Halloween makeup. You may want to invite parent helpers for this activity.

- Students can make clown hats by forming a cone with paper, then stapling it together. They can decorate the hats with paint, glitter, markers and stickers. Instead of wearing the hats, some students may want to draw faces on balloons and put the clown hats on them!

Extension Activities

⚠ Host your own "Greatest Show on Earth" in your classroom. Charge small coins for students to count out for an entrance fee. Invite students to display their talents in a variety of circus events and activities. Choose an area for the "main ring" (large area rug) and other parts of the room for sideshows (in smaller rings such as "Hoola-Hoops™") or exhibits and booths. Set up booths manned by parent volunteers. Serve peanuts or popcorn in bags and "sell" hot dogs and soda. Involve many people including parents and older students as clowns or magicians. Ask students to bring real animals in cages or stuffed animal toys to show off as exhibits. Provide inexpensive prizes.

Under the Big Top

⚠ Bake sugar cookies, then let students add clown-face details with chocolate chips, raisins, licorice and candies.

⚠ Students will enjoy making clown "cone-heads." Scoop vanilla ice cream in a dish and top it with a sugar cone "cap." Canned whipped cream can be sprayed around the cone for hair, and candies and peanuts can be clown-face features.

Under the Big Top

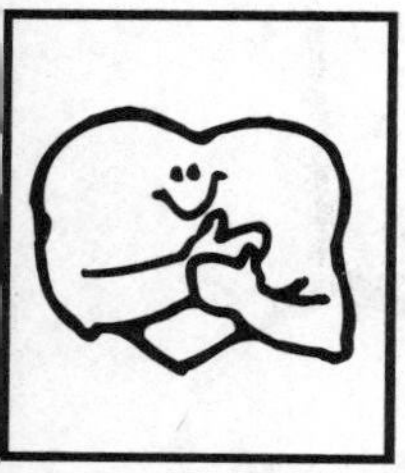

Values Education Experience

- Lead a discussion on appropriate times and places to "clown around." When is such behavior inappropriate?

April Showers Day

April 4

Setting the Stage

- Display an open umbrella with books all around it. Add the caption: "April Showers Bring Reading Hours." To turn this into a bulletin board, simply use a picture of an umbrella with book jackets around it.

- Hang student stories on paper raindrops from an open umbrella. Punch a hole in each story and thread dental floss through it. Hang it from a metal divider on the umbrella. See pattern on page 37.

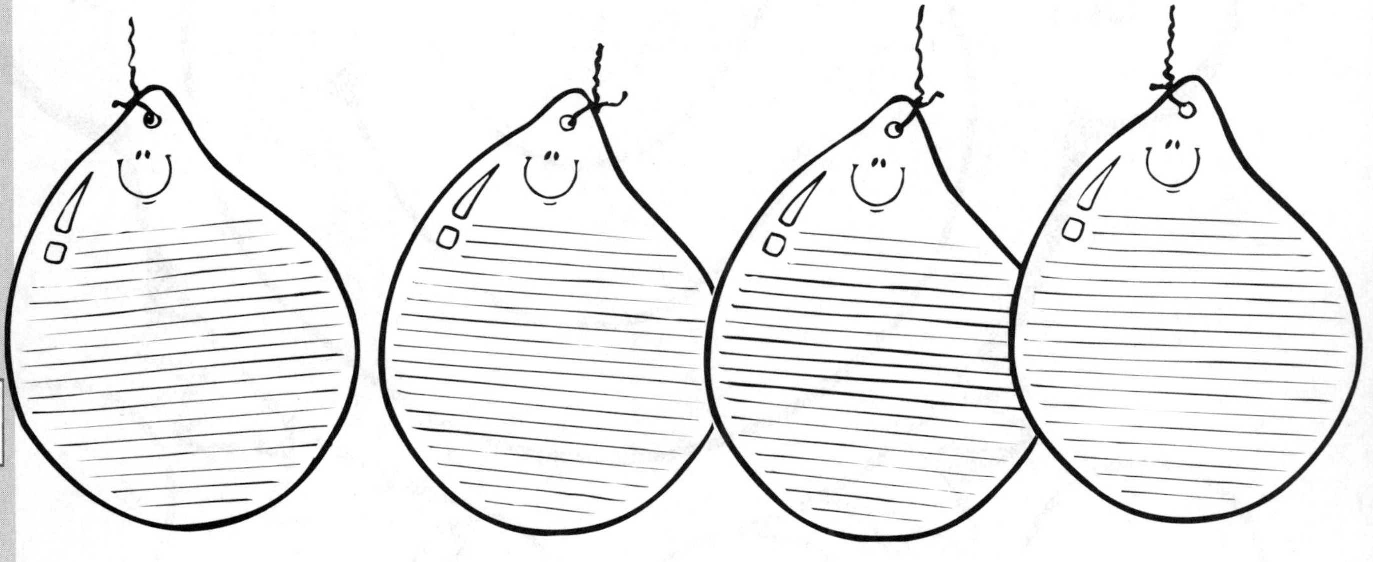

- Invite the students ahead of time to bring umbrellas to school today. Desks can be moved apart and open umbrellas can divide them. If it rains today, you'll be prepared for a class walk in the rain!

- Construct a semantic map or web with facts your students know (or want to know) about rain.

Historical Background

April usually is a rainy month throughout much of the United States causing the familiar saying, "April Showers Bring May Flowers!"

Literary Exploration

After the Rain by Norma Fox Mazer
April Showers by George Shannon, et al
Cloudy with a Chance of Meatballs by Judi Barrett
Huff and Puff's April Showers by Jean Warren
It Chanced to Rain by Kathleen Bullock
Listen to the Rain by Bill Martin, Jr.
My Red Umbrella by Robert Bright
Noah's Ark by Peter Spier
One Rainy Day by Valeri Gorbachev
Peter Spier's Rain by Peter Spier
Rain by David Bennett
Rain by Robert Kalan
Rain by Manya Stojic
The Rain Cloud by Mary Rayner
Rain Drop Splash by Alvin Tresselt
Rain Makes Applesauce by Julian Scheer
Rain Rain Rivers by Uri Shulevitz
Rain Song by Lezlie Evans
Rain Talk by Mary Serfozo
The Rainbabies by Laura Krauss Melmed
Richard Scarry's Best Rainy Day Book Ever by Richard Scarry
Sun, Rain by Niki Yektai
That Sky, That Rain by Carolyn Otto
The Umbrella Day by Nancy Evans Cooney
The Yellow Umbrella by Henrik Drescher
Umbrella by Taro Yashima
Umbrella Parade by Kathy Feczko
We Hate Rain! by James Stevenson
Wet World by Norma Simon
When the Rain Stops by Sheila Cole

Writing Experience

- Have students imagine having adventures as raindrops. Let them write their stories on raindrop shapes. Hang them from the ceiling when they're done or use the reproducible on page 38.

Science/Health Experience

- Study the water cycle. First make a homemade cloud! Breathe onto a mirror and explain how the surface of the mirror is colder than the water vapor of your breath (which condenses to tiny water droplets). This is basically what happens with clouds in the sky. To show how evaporation works, put a small amount of water in a pan and heat it on a hot plate or leave it on a sunny windowsill. Go back in a little while and check the amount of water in the pan. Show how it has evaporated into the air. Explain that every day millions of tiny drops of water rise into the air (from bodies of water) and form clouds. If the drops of water become too big or make the cloud too heavy, they fall back to the Earth as rain. Water that is not soaked into the ground drains into bodies of water such as rivers and lakes and starts the whole process again.

Science/Health Experience continued

- Students can observe what happens when they put $1/2$ cup of water (like the water in a lake) in a zip-close plastic bag by a sunny windowsill. The water begins to evaporate and forms droplets on the sides of the bag which float down to the bottom again (like rain).
- Investigate together what the term *acid rain* means and what we can do about it.

Social Studies Experience

- Research areas of the world that have seasons of heavy rain. What are these rainy seasons called? Have students locate these areas on a world map. What do they have in common?

Music/Dramatic Experience

- Sing "How Many Raindrops?" (words and music by Trudi Behar) or "It Is Raining" (by Susan Widdifield from *Piggyback Songs*).

Physical/Sensory Experience

- Plan some rainy-day relays your class can do when outside activities are not an option. Let students suggest some of their own ideas and demonstrate them.

Arts/Crafts Experience

- Make Indian rainsticks, instruments used in many cultures throughout the world. Students paint paper towel tubes bright, vivid colors. When they're dry, students fill the tubes with toothpicks or rice. They secure construction paper circles around both ends with thick rubber bands to close them. Then they turn them upside down to hear the sound of rain!

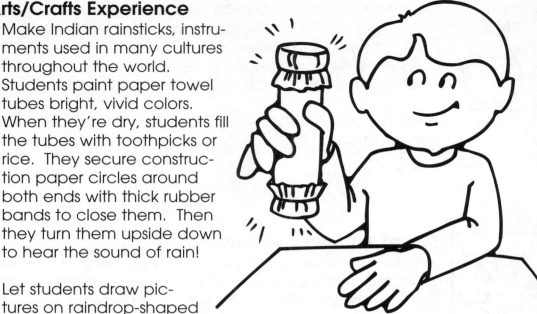

- Let students draw pictures on raindrop-shaped art paper of things they like to do on a rainy day. Each rainy day picture can be covered with blue cellophane to simulate rain "outside."

- Students can color rainy-day scenes, then add blue marker "raindrops." Then they carefully dip their pictures in clear water so the raindrops "run."

- Students can use upside down cupcake liners for umbrellas and raindrops cut from aluminum foil in their rainy-day pictures.

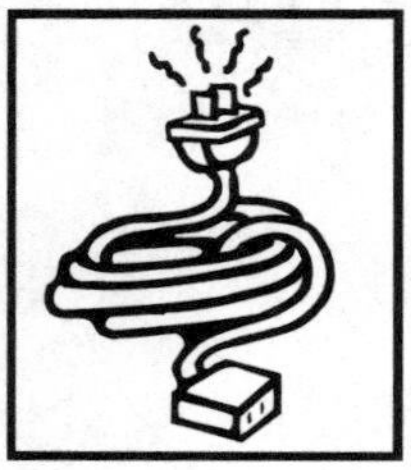

Extension Activities

- Have students each make a rain gauge to collect rain samples. They cut off the top portion of a two-liter plastic soda bottle and place it upside-down in the remaining portion so the funnel-shaped top is at the bottom. Then they tape a clear plastic ruler to the bottom so measurements can be made. Put one of these rain gauges outside (securing it so it is not disturbed) and let the rain fall. After each rain, mark the water level and record the data on a class chart.

⚠ Don't forget to celebrate worms and mud puddles at this time of year! Whip up some chocolate pudding, spoon it into paper cups, add chocolate cookie crumbs for dirt and a gummy worm! Let each student make one.

⚠ Serve cupcakes with "sprinkles" (of sugar, not rain).

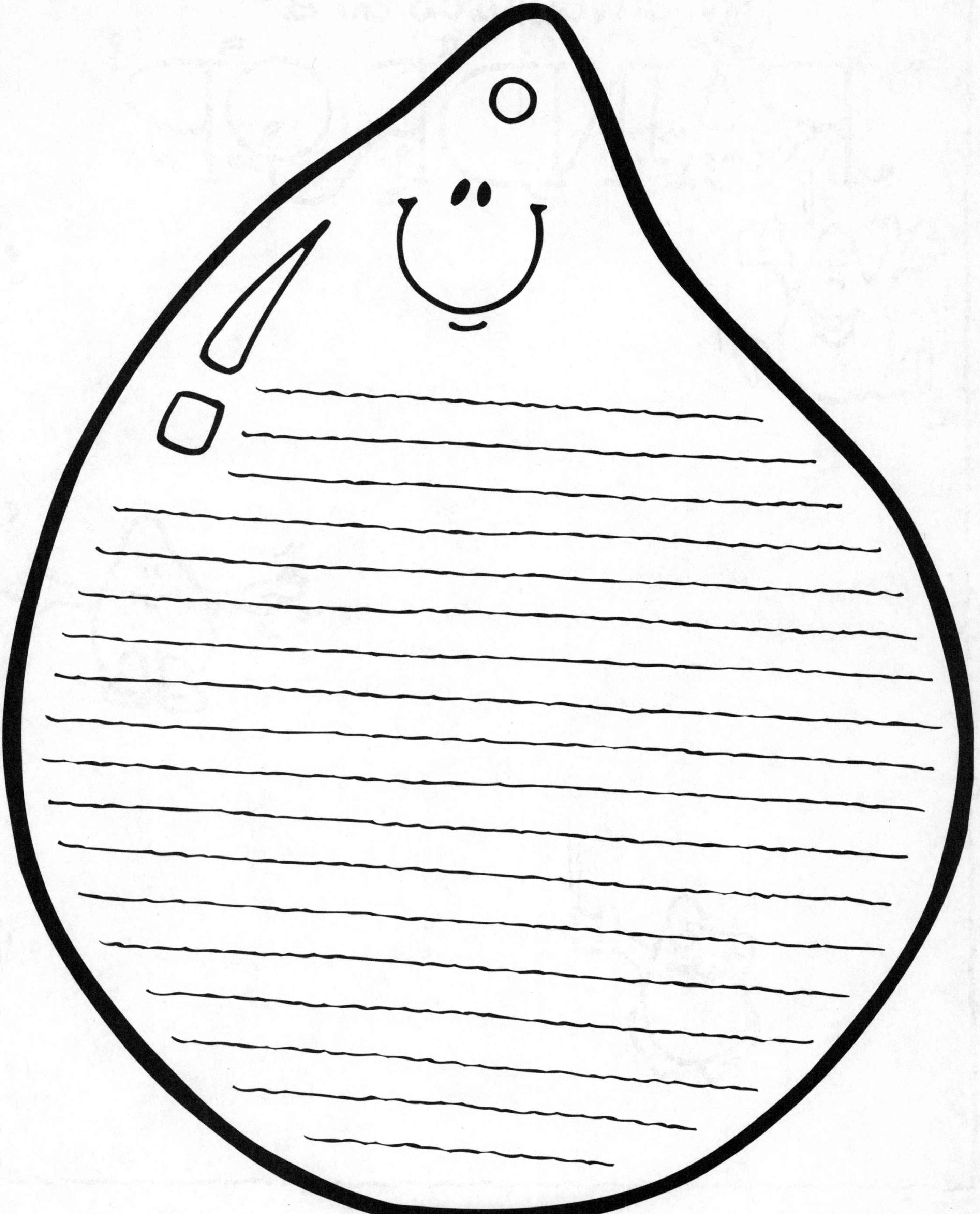

My adventures as a RAINDROP

Name:

Good-Bye, Germs Day

April 5

Setting the Stage

- Construct a semantic web with facts your students know (or would like to know) about germs and how they are spread.

Historical Background

The English physician, Sir Joseph Lister, was born on this day in 1827. He is famous for his work of pioneering surgical procedures. In the early 1800s, germs were actually being spread from doctors and unclean instruments to patients. The mortality rate was often 50% or more. Lister introduced antiseptics and sterilization during surgical procedures, and the mortality rate dropped to about 2%.

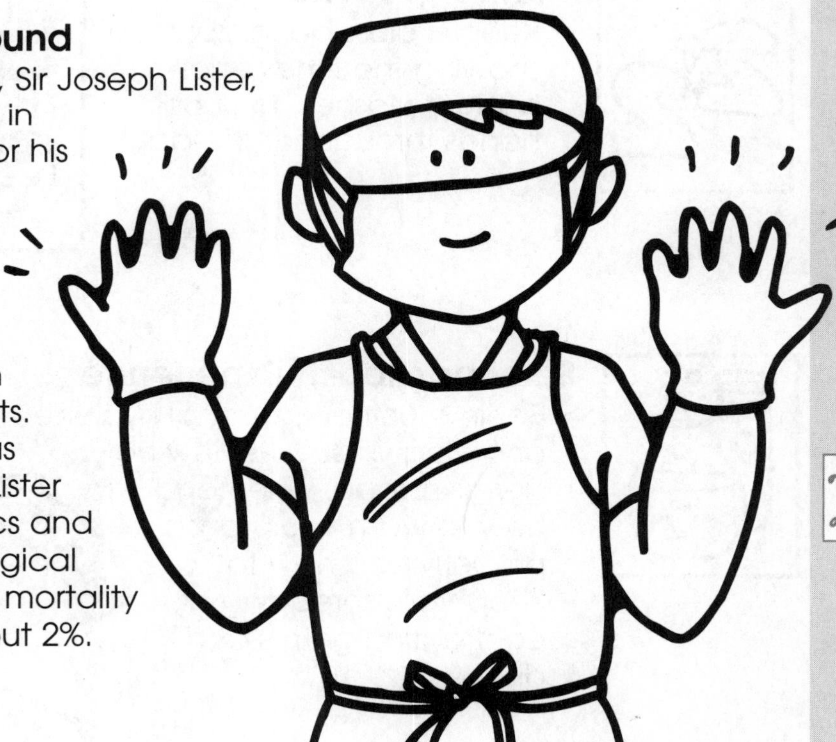

Literary Exploration

Body Battles by Rita Golden Gelman
Germs! by Dorothy Hinshaw Patent
Germs Make Me Sick! by Melvin Berger
Germs Make Me Sick: A Health Handbook for Kids by Parnell Donahue
How Did We Find Out About Germs? by Isaac Asimov
No Bath Tonight by Jane Yolen

Writing Experience

- Ask students to imagine they are "germs." They can write about their adventures during a day in the life of a germ. See reproducible on page 43.

Math Experience

- Keep a class bar graph showing the times each student washes his or her hands throughout the day.

Science/Health Experience

- Begin a unit on personal hygiene and cleanliness. Review how germs spread, when and how to wash your hands properly and how to keep from spreading or contracting germs and disease.

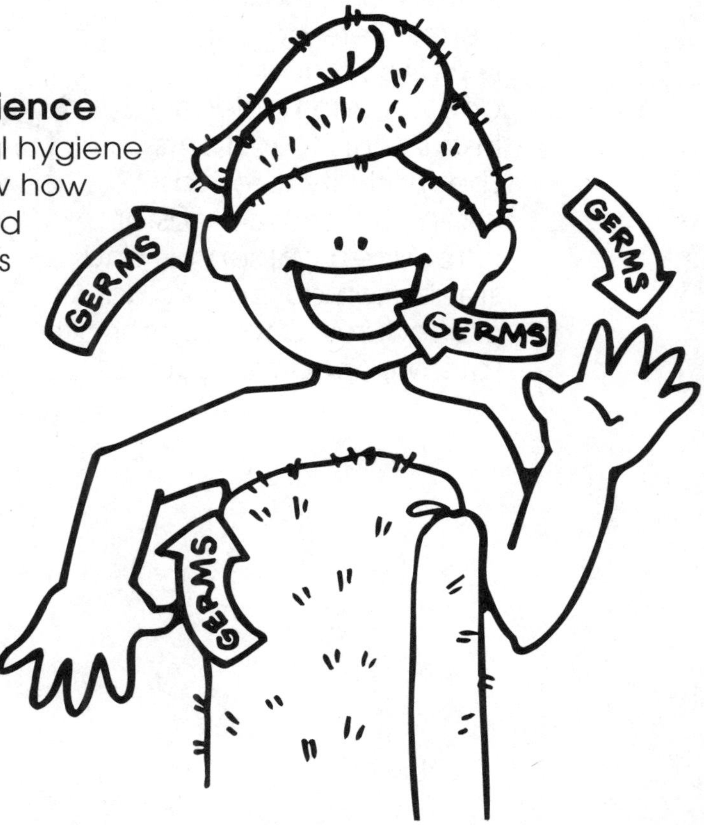

Social Studies Experience

- Learn about the history of medical and surgical procedures before and after Joseph Lister's important work.

Music/Dramatic Experience

- Let students invent a new brand or kind of soap, then advertise it to make people want to buy it.

- Illustrate with an atomizer spray bottle how sneezing spreads germs. As the children say, "Ahh-choo!" they spray water from the bottle to feel and see what happens during a sneeze. Reinforce the need for covering sneezes with tissues.

Physical/Sensory Experience

- Play Germ Wars! Divide students into two teams and have them form real or imaginary borders. At your signal, students throw foam balls at each other. Anyone hit with a foam ball (germ), falls to the ground as if very sick, lying there until another student on the team, a "Doctor Lister," gives him or her a "shot" (a light touch) with a foam or waffle bat. Students can aim their "germs" at the doctor of the opposing team. If the doctor is hit, no one can give shots, so the other team automatically wins.

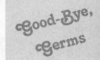

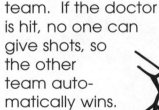

Arts/Crafts Experience

- Try some Sniffle Art! Let students draw self-portraits. Then have each trace around a hand and cut it out. They can place a real tissue in the hand and glue both over the mouth and nose of the portrait.

Extension Activities

- Take your class to visit a hospital and observe a surgery center. Perhaps a physician's assistant could explain to your students the importance of cleanliness in the operating room.

Follow-Up/Homework Idea

- Encourage students to keep track of their personal hygiene at home (washing hands, brushing teeth, taking a bath or shower) for a week.

If I were a GERM...

Olympic Games Day

April 6

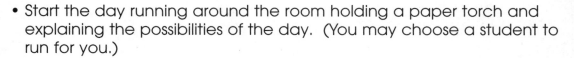

Setting the Stage

- Display student work around Olympic rings with the caption: "Gold Medal Work!" or "Go for the Gold!" (The rings should be positioned with the blue, black and red rings on the top row and the yellow and green below, linked in between.)

- Start the day running around the room holding a paper torch and explaining the possibilities of the day. (You may choose a student to run for you.)

Setting the Stage continued

- Let students make flags to represent different countries. They can fly them at their desks stuck in clay or in pint milk cartons.

- Construct a semantic web with facts your students know about the Olympic Games. Work together on a list of questions about the Olympic Games they would like answered during the course of the day.

Historical Background

The first modern Olympic Games took place on this day in 1896 in Athens, Greece, with 13 countries represented. The purpose behind the Olympic events was to bring countries together in peace and friendship and encourage excellence in sports.

Literary Exploration

The Animal Olympics by Howard Everett Smith
The Mud Flat Olympics by James Stevenson
The Olympics by Jane Duden
Olympics by Dennis Fradin
The Olympics by Peter Tatlow
The Summer Olympics by Caroline Arnold

Language Experience

- As a class, brainstorm Olympic events (running, long jump, discus, javelin, wrestling, boxing, fencing, rowing, swimming, archery, gymnastics and so on). Have students alphabetize the list.

Writing Experience

- Ask students to imagine that the Olympic judges are tired of all the regular events and need ideas for a new one. Ask each student to write a proposal for a new Olympic event. See reproducible on page 51.

Math Experience

- If students are involved in classroom Olympic events today (see page 48), let them measure distances achieved in the long jump, discus and javelin throws.

Social Studies Experience

- Students can research Olympic champions and add the names to a class time line of the Olympic Games. Pinpoint which country each champion represented.

- Have students research Olympic symbols such as the Olympic motto, creed, flag, flame and oath.

Music/Dramatic Experience

- Invite students to imagine they have won Olympic medals. Invite them to give "Olympic acceptance speeches."

Physical/Sensory Experience

- Host your own classroom Olympic Games! Set up areas for an obstacle course, long jump, discus throw (with a Frisbee™ or paper plate), javelin throw (with a paper straw) and shot put (with a Nerf™ ball).

Arts/Crafts Experience

- Ask students to draw themselves competing as summer Olympic athletes in their favorite events.

Extension Activities

⚠ Represent America by serving patriotic cupcakes! Attach a miniature American flag to each cupcake.

⚠ Serve Torch Treats, orange sherbet in cones.

- Make paper Olympic medals and give one to every student who participates in the day's activities. See patterns on pages 49-50.

Values Education Experience

- Many Olympic champions overcame great personal challenges to participate in the Olympic Games. Runner Wilma Rudolph had polio which crippled her left leg. Discuss the value of perseverance and determination to overcome obstacles and not let them stand in our way.

Follow-Up/Homework Idea

- Challenge students to be academic Olympians, giving their best in everything they do.

OLYMPIC
GOOD SPORT

OLYMPIC
GOOD SPORT

OLYMPIC
GOOD SPORT

OLYMPIC
PARTICIPANT

OLYMPIC
PARTICIPANT

PROPOSAL

for a new Olympic event!

World Health Day

April 7

Setting the Stage

- Display some fruit, a jump rope, a pillow and a box of tissues around health-related literature.

- Construct a semantic web with facts your students know about keeping healthy. Then list questions they would like answered about health throughout the day.

Historical Background

The World Health Organization was founded on this day in 1948 and this date was officially declared World Health Day.

Literary Exploration

The Body by Lionel Bender
Care for Your Body! by Rhoda Nottridge
The Don't Spoil Your Body Book by Claire Rayner
Inside You and Me by Eloise Turner and Carroll Fenton
The Magic School Bus Inside the Human Body by JoAnna Cole
See How You Grow by Patricia Pearse
Stay Fit: Build a Strong Body by Catherine Reef
You and Your Food by Judy Tatchell and Dilys Wells

Writing Experience

- Let students imagine they have secret recipes passed down from their grandmas which are sure cures for what ails ya'! Have them write about "Granny's Old-Time Cure-All." See reproducible on page 55.

Science/Health Experience

- Begin a unit of study on maintaining a healthy life-style.

Music/Dramatic Experience

- Have students role-play situations which require them to make health-related choices. (Example: A student at home is hungry. He sees pieces of fruit or chocolate cake in the kitchen. What would the student do and why?)

World Health

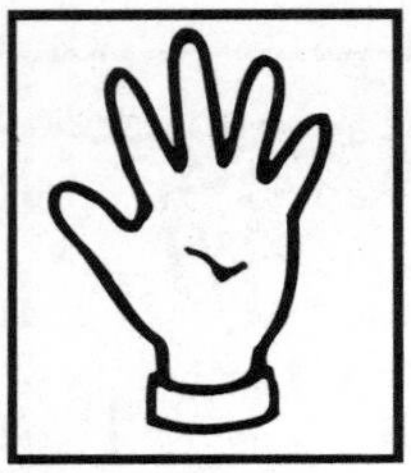

Physical/Sensory Experience

- Encourage better health with classroom fitness exercises! Do a few jumping jacks or sit-ups or run in place!

Arts/Crafts Experience

- Let students cut pictures out of magazines and make collages of good health practices (people resting, getting exercise and eating nutritious food).

Extension Activities

- Take your class to visit a doctor's office or invite a doctor to come and speak to your students about how they can be healthier.

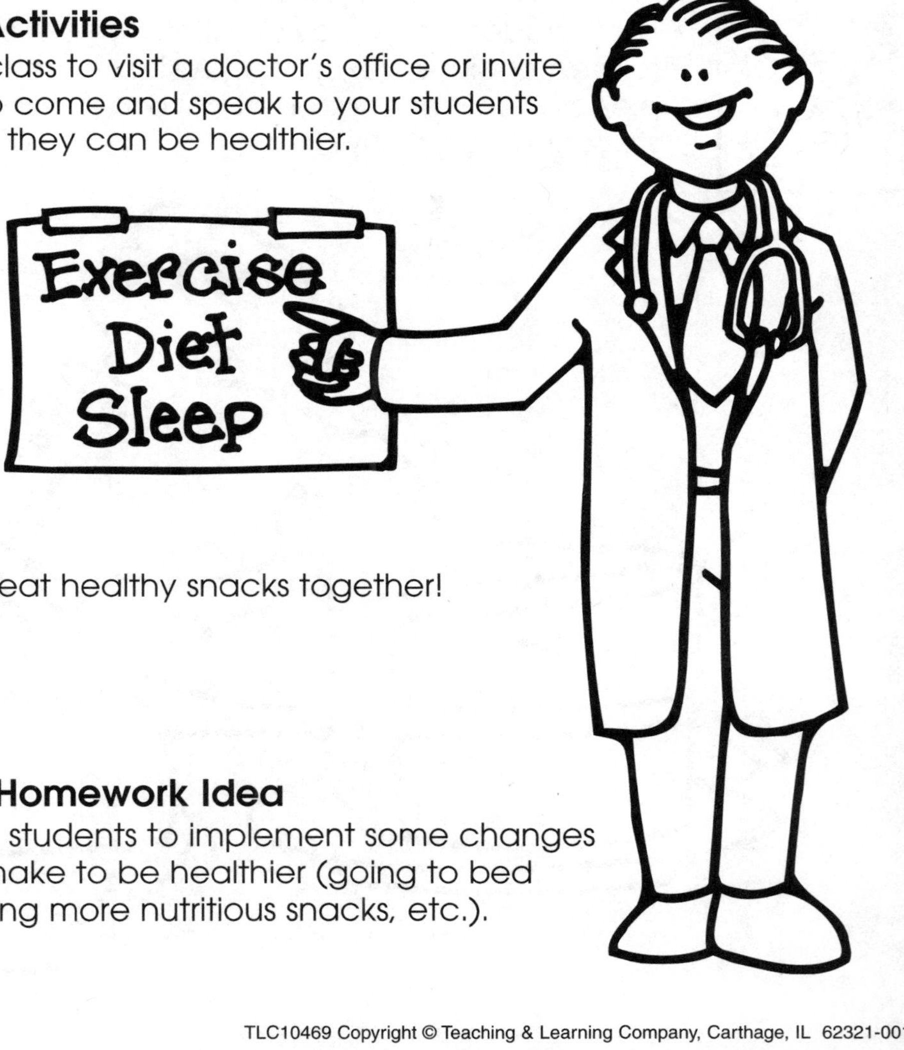

- Make and eat healthy snacks together!

Follow-Up/Homework Idea

- Encourage students to implement some changes they can make to be healthier (going to bed earlier, eating more nutritious snacks, etc.).

Granny's Old-Time Cure-All

Name:

Castle Creations Day

April 8

Setting the Stage

- Display old looking goblets and a crown. Invite all your knights and damsels to the "Round Table." Add related literature to get students excited about today's activities.

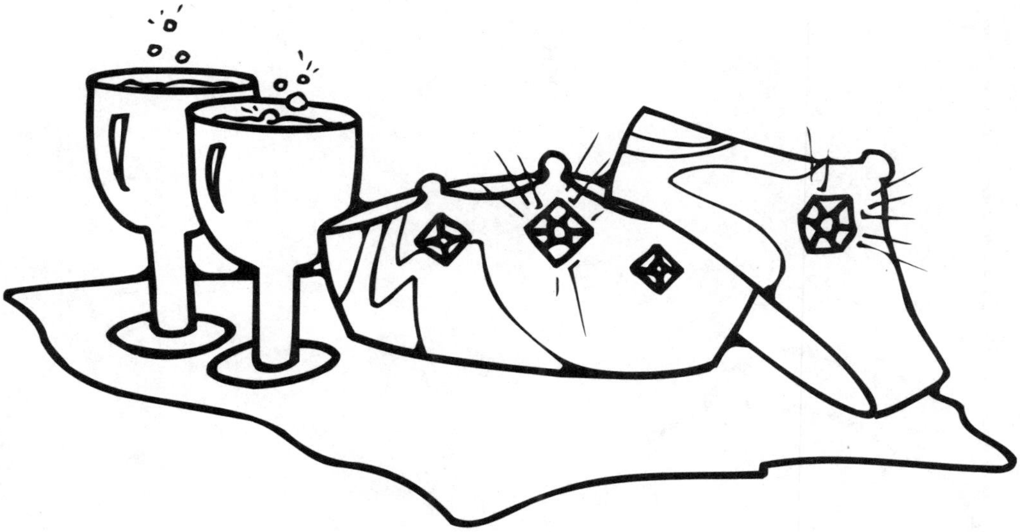

- Construct a semantic web with facts your students know about castles. Ask them to help you list things they would like to learn about castles today.

Literary Exploration

Castle by David MacCaulay
The Castle Builder by Dennis Nolan
Castles by Fon Wyman Boardman
Creepy Castle by John S. Goodall
Half a Kingdom: An Iceland Folktale by Ann McGovern, et al
King Bidgood's in the Bathtub by Audrey and Don Wood
The King's Chessboard by David Birch

Literary Exploration continued

The King's Equal by Katherine Paterson
Knights of the Kitchen Table by Jon Scieszka
Many Moons by James Thurber
Medieval Feast by Aliki
The Midnight Castle by Consuelo Joerns
My Castle by Florence Parry Heide
Nora's Castle by Satomi Ichikawa
The Ordinary Princess by M.M. Kaye
The Prince and the Pink Blanket by Barbara Brenner
The Prince's Tooth Is Loose by Harriet Ziefert
St. George and the Dragon by Margaret Hodges
The Story of a Castle by John S. Goodall
There's No Such Dragon by Jack Kent

Writing Experience

- Ask students to imagine that they are brave knights riding off into battle to protect a castle. Have them write about their adventures. See reproducible on page 60.

Math Experience

- If you make homemade castles today (see below), have students measure the towers and drawbridges.

Social Studies Experience

- Learn about castles (past and present). Your students may not realize that there are still castles all over the world, particularly in Europe. Find some pictures of castles in Great Britain, Germany or France.

Music/Dramatic Experience

- Let students act out or role-play imaginary scenes from King Arthur's Court.

Physical/Sensory Experience

- Let students "joust" with foam bats.

- Let students role-play different Medieval people and let other students guess who they are (knight in heavy armor, knight on horseback, lady dancing, farmer, blacksmith, etc.).

Arts/Crafts Experience

- Divide students into groups and let them work together to make castles out of oatmeal containers, cardboard boxes, construction paper, cardboard tubes and craft materials. Then cut out people (and a dragon) to live in the castles.

Arts/Crafts Experience continued

- See patterns for castle action figures on pages 61-63.

Extension Activities

⚠ Make an Edible Castle! Remove the box around a half-gallon of ice cream. Place the rectangle ice cream box shape on a plate and add a sugar cone "tower" to each corner. Let students decorate the castle with nuts, candies or fruit. Then let each one have a slice of the royal life!

Follow-Up/Homework Idea

- Tell students to go straight home to their castles and enjoy a family meal at their own round or square tables.

If I were a KNIGHT...

Name:

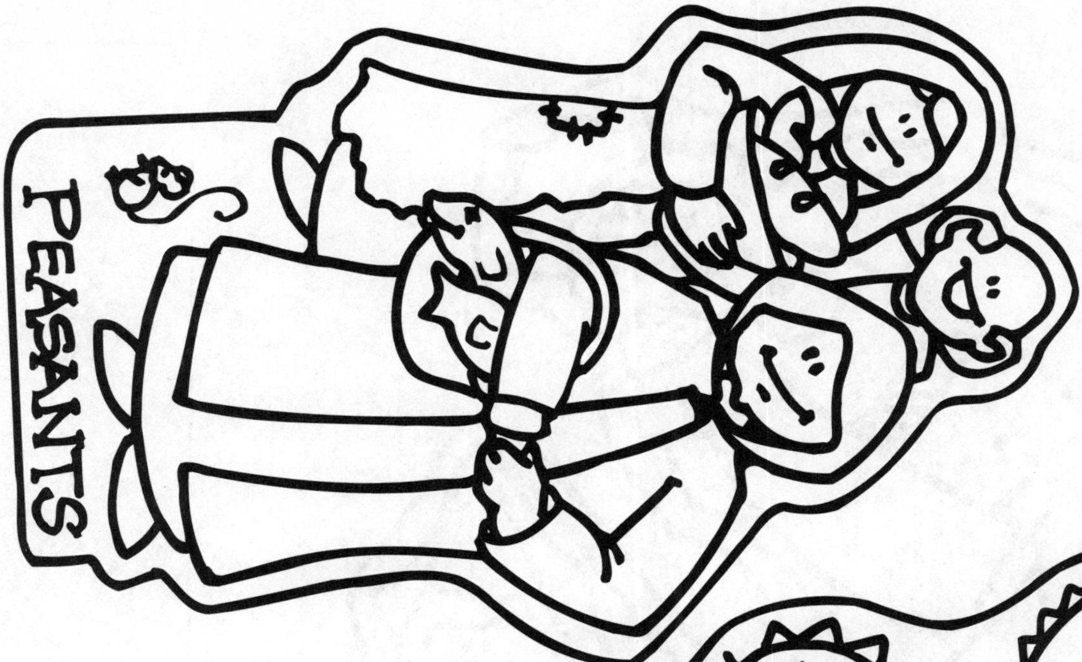
PEASANTS

KNIGHT

DRAGON

KING

DAMSEL

QUEEN

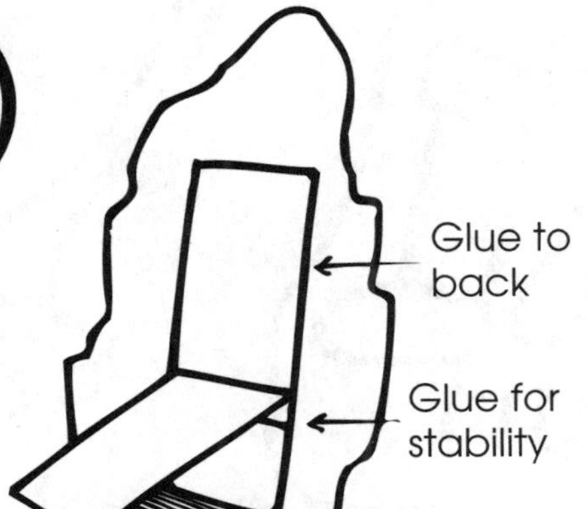
Glue to back
Glue for stability

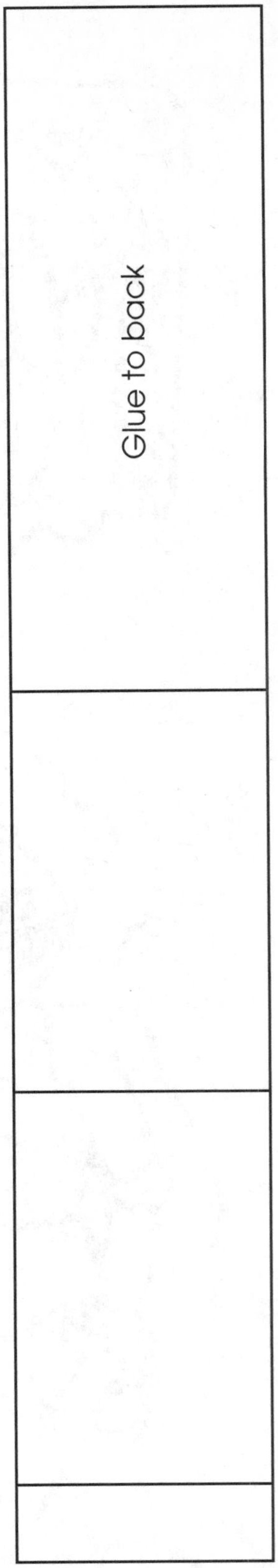
Glue to back

Glue to back	Glue to back	Glue to back	Glue to back	Glue to back

Library Day

April 9

Setting the Stage

- Display pictures of libraries around some of your students' favorite library books.

- Construct a semantic web with facts your students know (or would like to know) about libraries to help you plan your day's activities.

Historical Background

America's first free library was opened to the public in Peterborough, New Hampshire. The citizens decided to use a portion of the town's taxes to support the library. This was the beginning of libraries being supported largely through taxes (although private donations often help subsidize them such as when Andrew Carnegie donated nearly 50 million dollars to support libraries all over the country).

Literary Exploration

Cannon the Librarian by Mike Thaler, et al
Check It Out!: The Book About Libraries by Gail Gibbons
I Can Be a Librarian by Carol Greene
The Library Dragon by Carmen Agra Deedy
The Librarian from the Black Lagoon by Mike Thaler
Something Queer at the Library by Elizabeth Levy

Writing Experience

- Encourage students to write thank-you letters to your school librarian. Compile them into a book to give the librarian in appreciation for all he or she does for the school. See reproducible on page 68.

Math Experience

- Let students measure the area, perimeter and weight of library books in your classroom.
- Have students estimate the number of pages in some books. Check to see whose estimate is the closest each time.

Science/Health Experience

- Challenge your students to find books in your school or classroom library that deal with science or health-related topics.

Social Studies Experience

- Study how libraries have evolved over the years. (Early libraries chained books to bookshelves and only wealthy men could visit them.)

- Find out where the largest library in the United States is. Locate the city on a U.S. map. How many books does it have?

Physical/Sensory Experience

- Brainstorm a list of items to scavenge in a library scavenger hunt. (Examples: a book about wind, a book about a war hero and a book about drawing cartoons) Set a time limit and let students try to find as many books on their list as possible.

Arts/Crafts Experience

- Let students make posters to hang around the school promoting use of the library.

GET
HOOKED
ON BOOKS!
Visit
your library!

Extension Activities

- Take your class for a visit to a public library for a tour.
- Invite your school librarian to visit your class to tell about his or her work with books.

Values Education Experience

- Discuss the value of reading good books. Encourage students to appreciate our country's library system that allows them to borrow books about anything in the universe!

Follow-Up/Homework Idea

- Ask students to count the number of books in their home library.

Library Day

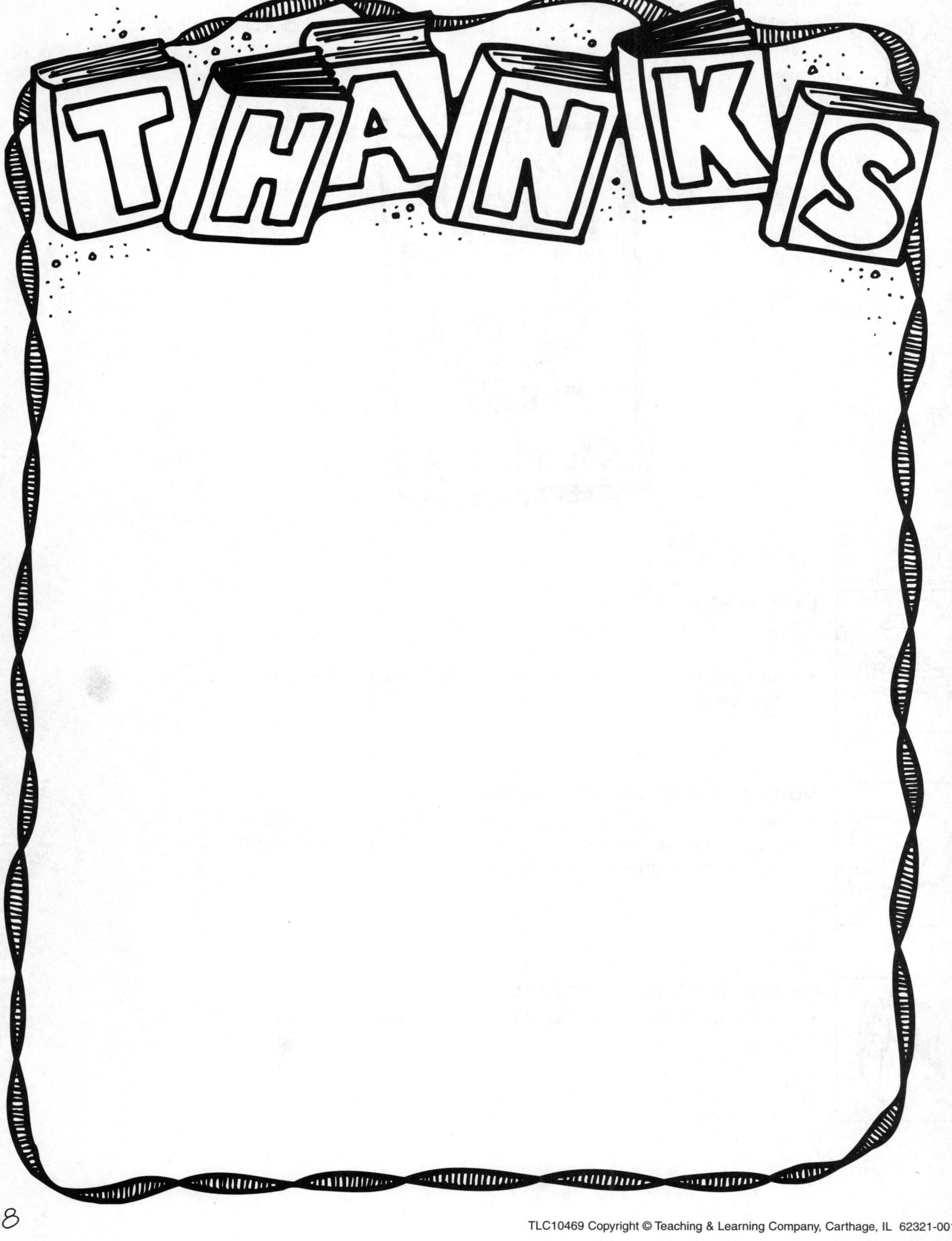
THANKS

Humane Day

April 10

Humane Day

Humane Day

Setting the Stage

- Construct a semantic web with words your students think of when you say the word *kindness.*

Historical Background

The Charter to incorporate the American Society for the Prevention of Cruelty to Animals was passed by the New York Legislature on this day in 1866. Henry Bergh, the founder of the ASPCA, brought global attention to the needs and rights of animals everywhere. Today, cruelty to animals is usually a punishable offense that can bring a hefty fine or time in jail.

Literary Exploration

Andy and the Lion: A Tale of Kindness Remembered by James Daugherty
Kids' Random Acts of Kindness by Rosalynn Carter, et al
Kindness by Jane Belk Moncure
Kindness (Learn the Value of series) by Elaine Goley
Random Acts of Kindness by Daphne Rose Kingma
The Value of Kindness by Spencer Johnson

Language Experience

- As a class, brainstorm acts of kindness.
- Write the word *humane* on the board. Ask students to tell what they think it means. What important word is a big part of *humane*? (human)

Writing Experience

- Ask students to write about what rights they think animals have. See reproducible on page 73.

- If you have a chance to visit a local pound or animal shelter today (see page 72), students can write articles for the school newspaper to help find homes for animals they see that need to be adopted.

Social Studies Experience

- Discuss what a humanitarian is. What constitutes a humanitarian relief effort? Ask students to point out places in the world where humanitarian relief efforts have been needed. Let them share what they know about the disasters.

Music/Dramatic Experience

- Students will enjoy role-playing pet-owners and pets. Have them demonstrate actions that show kindness and care to pets (petting, feeding, a soft tone of voice, etc.).

Physical/Sensory Experience

- Make a Kindness Tree! Spray-paint a tree branch white and "plant" it in a container or trash can filled with raffia or leftover Easter grass. Dip cotton balls in dry pink tempera paint and hang them on the tree for blossoms. If students brainstormed acts of kindness earlier in the day (see page 70), have them write some on slips of paper and put them next to the tree. As students carry out these kind acts throughout the day, they can attach the paper slips to the branches. What a great way to encourage kindness in and out of the classroom!

Arts/Crafts Experience

- Students can draw pictures of the animals they see in the shelter or local pound that need homes. If you aren't able to visit the animals, ask the workers to provide detailed descriptions of them so your students can draw their pictures and help find good, loving homes for them.

Humane Day

Extension Activities

- Take a field trip to a local animal shelter or invite a representative from the pound to visit your class to talk about the efforts made to save animals and provide good homes for them.

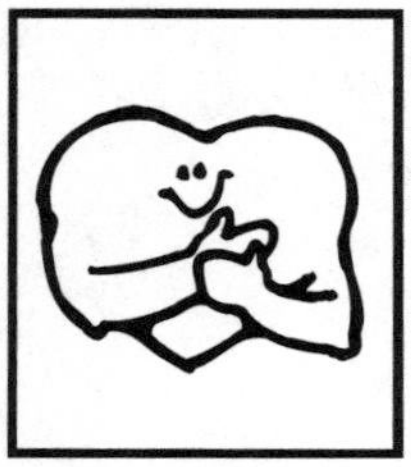

Values Education Experience

- Author George Eliot said, "Animals are such agreeable friends; they ask no questions, pass no criticisms." Discuss what that means. Ask students with pets to share how they are good friends. Discuss what we can learn from our pets about accepting one another.

Humane Day

Follow-Up/Homework Idea

- Encourage students to show kindness to all living things wherever they are.

WE HAVE RIGHTS
GET OUT OF YOUR SHELL & GIVE US SUPPORT!
SQUEAK UP FOR Kindness

100th Day of the Year

April 11

Setting the Stage

- Create an atmosphere of festivity by displaying balloons and party paraphernalia all around the room. Hang a big sign or write across the board, "Celebrating Our 100th Day of the Year!"

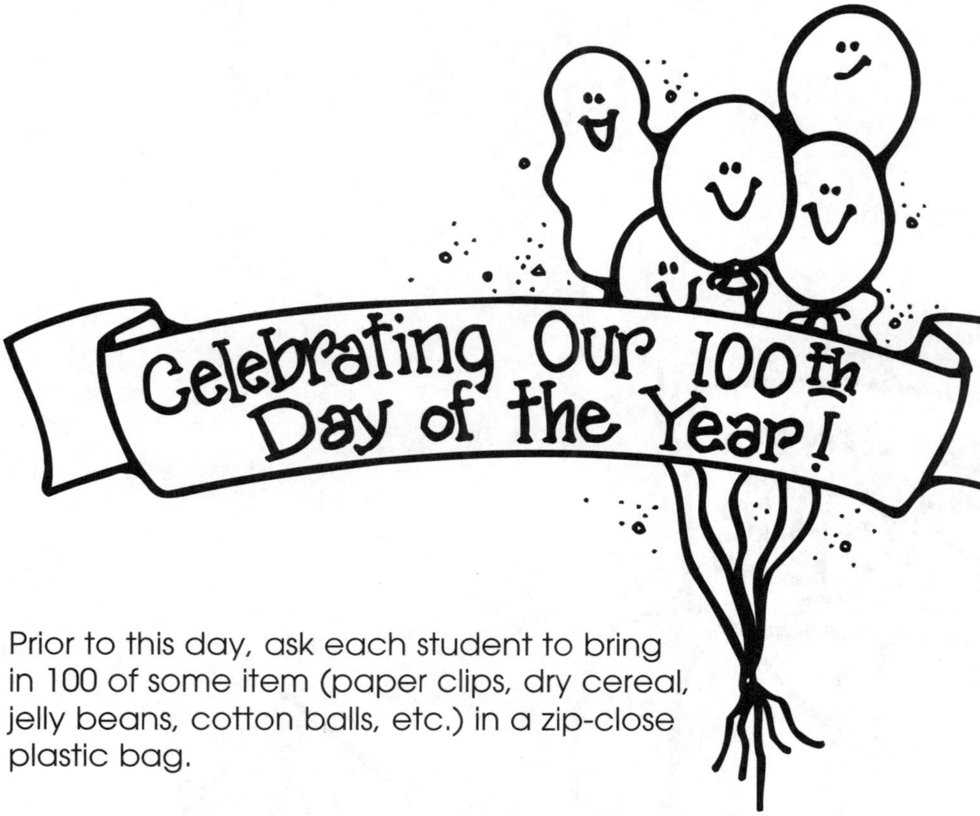

- Prior to this day, ask each student to bring in 100 of some item (paper clips, dry cereal, jelly beans, cotton balls, etc.) in a zip-close plastic bag.

Historical Background

April 11th is the 100th day of the current year! What a great reason to celebrate!

Literary Exploration

Counting Our Way to the 100th Day! by Betsy Franco
I'll Teach My Dog 100 Words by Michael Frith
The 100th Day of School by Angela Shelf Medearis
The 100th Day of School! by Matt Mitter
The Hundredth Name by Shulamith Levey Oppenheim

Language Experience

- Ask students to grab books and find the 100th page. Ask them to read the page and imagine what happened before and what will happen after that page.

- Encourage students to practice spelling 100 words from a grade level sight word list. Give a spelling test and certificates that states that they know at least 100 of their ________ (fill in grade) words! See award patterns on page 78.

Writing Experience

- As a follow-up to the 100th page activity, ask students to write what they think happened either before or after the 100th page. See reproducible on page 79.

- Ask your students to imagine they are someone else (the principal, their teacher, a parent or a famous person). If that person could have 100 of anything, what would it be and why? Have them write from those people's perspectives.

Math Experience

- Ask students to count the items they brought from home (page 74). Then let them have fun estimating and setting aside different amounts (53, 86, etc.). They can check their answers by counting the items set aside. Let them trade items and use a variety of them to create sequences.

- Students can group their items in groups of two, five and ten.

- Let students measure with centimeter and inch rulers how far across a desk their 100 items (end-to-end) stretch.

- Challenge students to use their calendars to figure out when the 100th day of school occurred.

Physical/Sensory Experience

- For fast finishers, set out a 100-piece puzzle to complete. Let them work on it together.

- Do a total of 100 physical exercises. Everyone works toward the total together (sit-ups, jumping rope, twirling a Hoola Hoop™, jumping jacks, etc.). Then get busy counting and exercising!

Arts/Crafts Experience

- Let students make mosaics from the 100 pieces they brought from home (page 74).

- Students can make, then decorate place mats with a number 100 in the center. They can use their place mats for the snack below. See place mat pattern on page 80.

Extension Activities

⚠ Give each student a breadstick half and two mini doughnuts so they can eat the number 100!

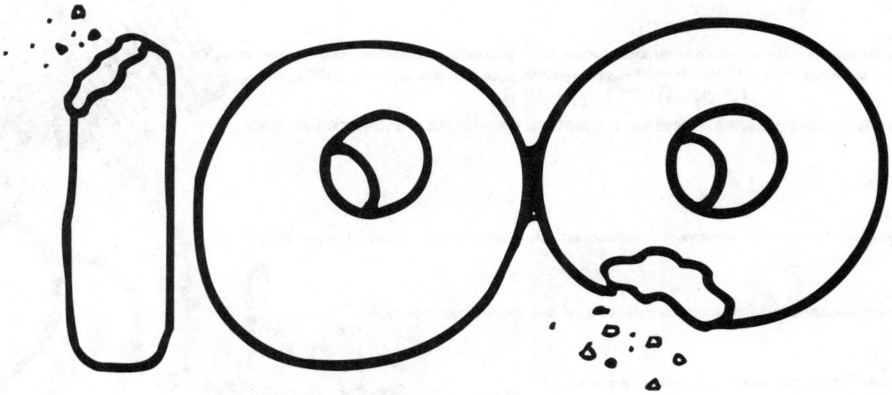

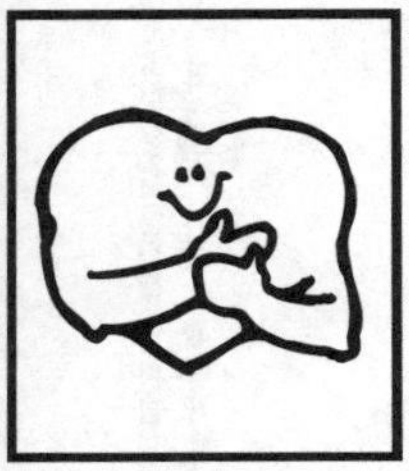

Values Education Experience

- Have students consider what it would be like to live to be 100 years old. What do they think will be most important to them when they reach 100?

Follow-Up/Homework Idea

- Ask students to count by hundreds on the way home.

CERTIFICATE

OF ACHIEVEMENT

awarded to: ______________________

for: ______________________

____

____

Teacher Signature

CERTIFICATE

OF ACHIEVEMENT

awarded to: ______________________

for: ______________________

____

____

Teacher Signature

What happened?

Beverly Cleary's Birthday

April 12

Setting the Stage

- Display all kinds of Beverly Cleary books to gather excitement for the day's activities.

Historical Background

Children's author, Beverly Cleary, was born on this day in 1916 in Oregon. She became popular for her Ramona book series and won a Newbery Medal for her book *Dear Mr. Henshaw*.

Literary Exploration

Beezus and Ramona by Beverly Cleary
Beverly Cleary by Julie Berg
Beverly Cleary: She Makes Reading Fun by Patricia Stone Martin
Dear Mr. Henshaw by Beverly Cleary
Ellen Tebbits by Beverly Cleary
Emily's Runaway Imagination by Beverly Cleary
Henry and Beezus by Beverly Cleary
Henry and Ribsy by Beverly Cleary
Henry and the Clubhouse by Beverly Cleary
Henry and the Paper Route by Beverly Cleary
Henry Huggins by Beverly Cleary

Literary Exploration continued

The Mouse and the Motorcycle by Beverly Cleary
Muggie Maggie by Beverly Cleary
Otis Spofford by Beverly Cleary
Petey's Bedtime Story by Beverly Cleary
Ralph S. Mouse by Beverly Cleary
Ramona and Her Father by Beverly Cleary
Ramona and Her Mother by Beverly Cleary
Ramona the Pest by Beverly Cleary
Ramona Quimby, Age 8 by Beverly Cleary
Ramona the Brave by Beverly Cleary
The Real Hole by Beverly Cleary
Ribsy by Beverly Cleary
Runaway Ralph by Beverly Cleary
Socks by Beverly Cleary
Two Dog Biscuits by Beverly Cleary

Language Experience

- Play Clothesline (like the Hangman game) by having students avoid adding articles of clothing to the clothesline and picking the correct letters in Cleary book titles.

Writing Experience

- After reading *Ramona the Pest* to your class, let them consider whether or not they are ever pests. Have them write their experiences. See reproducible on page 85.

- Challenge students to write poems about their favorite Beverly Cleary characters.

Are you a little
PEST?
Why or why not?
Name:

Math Experience

- Let students take a survey of other students' choices for favorite Beverly Cleary books. Add the information to a class bar graph.

Social Studies Experience

- Have students research Beverly Cleary's life. To get them started, tell them that her birthplace was McMinnville, Oregon, she was a librarian before writing children's books and she was the mother of twins.

Music/Dramatic Experience

- Divide students into groups and let them choose scenes from favorite Beverly Cleary books to act out.

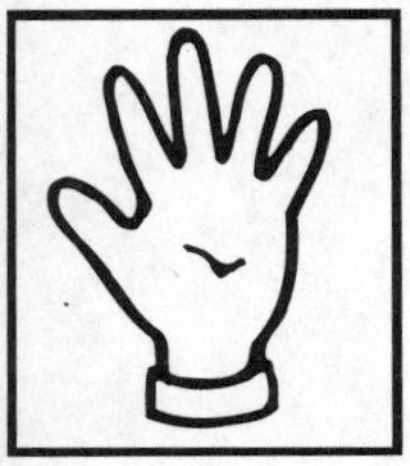

Physical/Sensory Experience

- After reading *Ramona the Pest*, let your students join Ramona in some kindergarten activities. They can play Duck, Duck Goose, do Ramona Seatwork, have Show and Tell, take an imaginary nap, have graham or zwieback crackers and milk, walk on tin-can stilts, etc. Borrow small chairs from a younger grade classroom to let students feel like kindergartners.

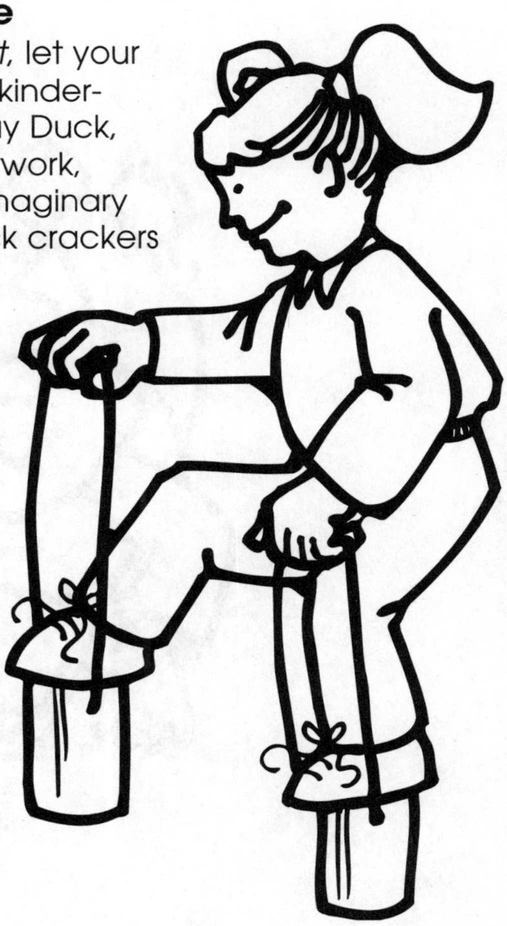

Arts/Crafts Experience

- After reading *Ramona and Her Father,* let each student take off a shoe and draw a sketch of one foot.

- Let students illustrate their favorite scene from a Beverly Cleary story, or work together on a Beverly Cleary mural.

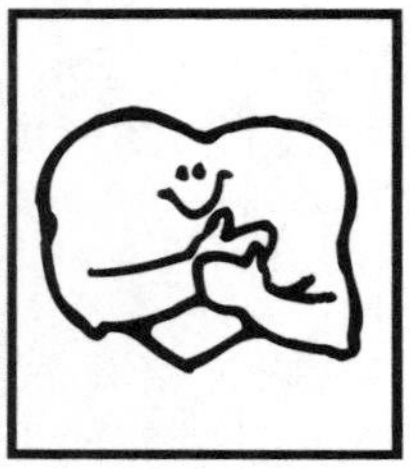

Values Education Experience

- When Beverly Cleary was young, she thought there weren't enough interesting, funny books for children to read. This was a factor in her decision to author children's books. Let students share important lessons they have learned from reading books.

Follow-Up/Homework Idea

- Encourage students to check out Beverly Cleary books to start reading at home tonight.

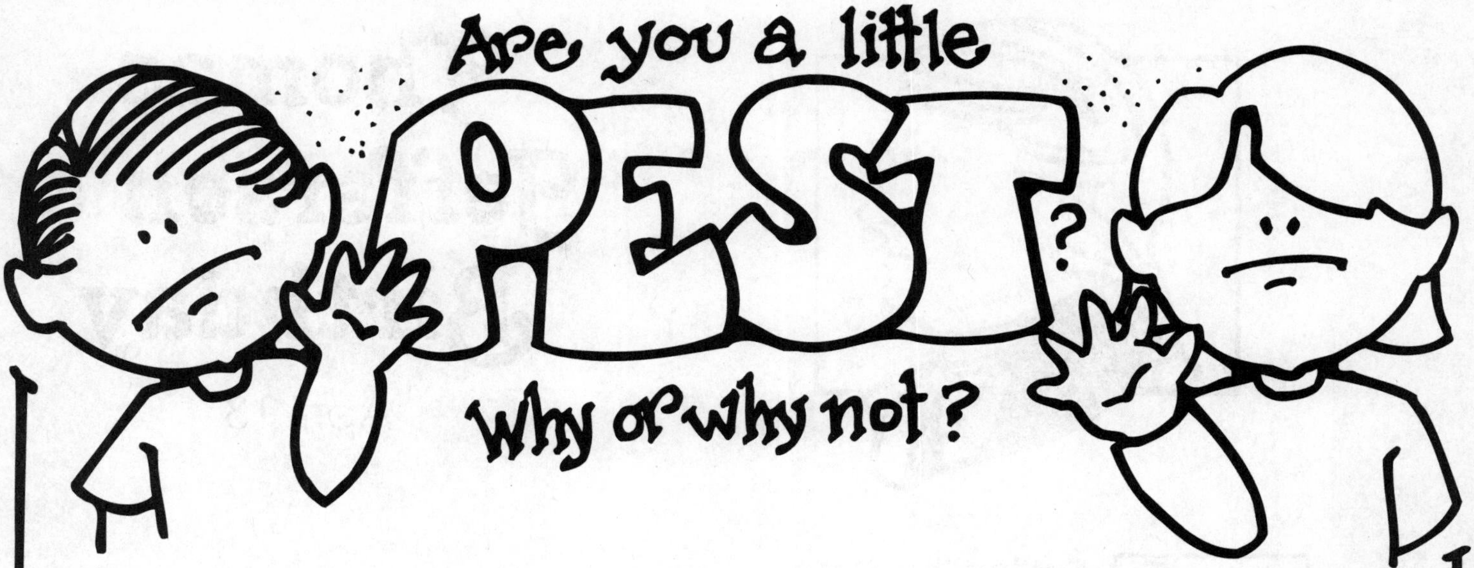
Are you a little
PEST?
Why or why not?

Name:

Thomas Jefferson's Birthday

April 13

Setting the Stage

- Display a copy of the Declaration of Independence and a blue or black tri-cornered patriot hat (found in novelty stores) around Jefferson-related literature.

- Construct a semantic web with facts your students know (or would like to know) about Thomas Jefferson.

Historical Background

Thomas Jefferson was born on this day in 1743 in Virginia. In 1801 he became the third President of the United States. He wrote the Declaration of Independence and founded the University of Virginia. Jefferson died in 1821.

Literary Exploration

Meet Thomas Jefferson by Marvin Barrett
Pass the Quill, I'll Write a Draft: A Story of Thomas Jefferson by Robert Quackenbush
Thomas Jefferson by Roger Bruns
Thomas Jefferson by Frank Hutchins
Thomas Jefferson by Susan Lee

Literary Exploration continued

Thomas Jefferson by Don Nardo
Thomas Jefferson by Charles Patterson
Thomas Jefferson by Kathie Billingslea Smith
Thomas Jefferson: Author, Inventor, President by Carol Greene
Thomas Jefferson: The Champion of the People by Clara Ingram Judson
Thomas Jefferson, the Complete Man by James Eichner
Thomas Jefferson: Man with a Vision by Ruth Crisman
The Value of Foresight: The Story of Thomas Jefferson by Ann Donegan Johnson
Young Thomas Jefferson by Francene Sabin

Language Experience

- Let students brainstorm how many words they can create from the letters in *Thomas Jefferson.*
- Have students suggest words to describe Thomas Jefferson's accomplishments. Print the words on the board.

Thomas Jefferson

Writing Experience

- Let students write personal "declarations of independence" asking parents for more independence (getting to stay up later at night or having extra privileges etc.).

Math Experience

- On what coin does Thomas Jefferson appear? Have students practice counting by fives.

Thomas Jefferson

Social Studies Experience

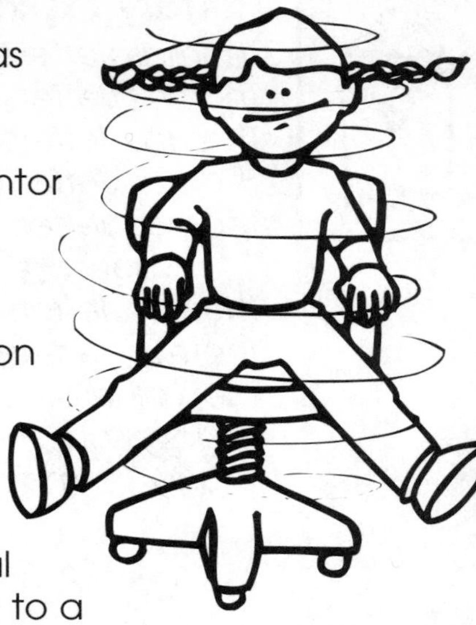

- Study the life and contributions of Thomas Jefferson (writer of the Declaration of Independence, governor of Virginia, founder of the University of Virginia, inventor of the polygraph, a swivel chair and decoding machine, and improving the plow for farmers). He also enjoyed botany, music and architecture. Jefferson died on the 50th anniversary of the Declaration of Independence (July 4th, 1826).

- Let students research significant historical events of this time period and add them to a class time line.

Music/Dramatic Experience

- Play patriotic music quietly in the background while students work on projects.

Thomas Jefferson

Arts/Crafts Experience

- Students can do coin rubbings of Jefferson's famous coin, the nickel. They can use the coin rubbings around the border of a handwriting assignment quoting Jefferson: "We hold these truths to be self-evident, that all men are created equal."

Thomas Jefferson

Extension Activities

⚠ Serve cold macaroni pasta in honor of Jefferson! He loved macaroni after sampling it in Paris, and had a macaroni machine brought from Italy so it could be served in the White House.

⚠ Thomas Jefferson was credited with the decision that white potatoes and tomatoes are edible. Before he stood up for them, people assumed that both were poisonous. Bake and serve Tater Tots™ with ketchup or some tomato slices for a healthy snack.

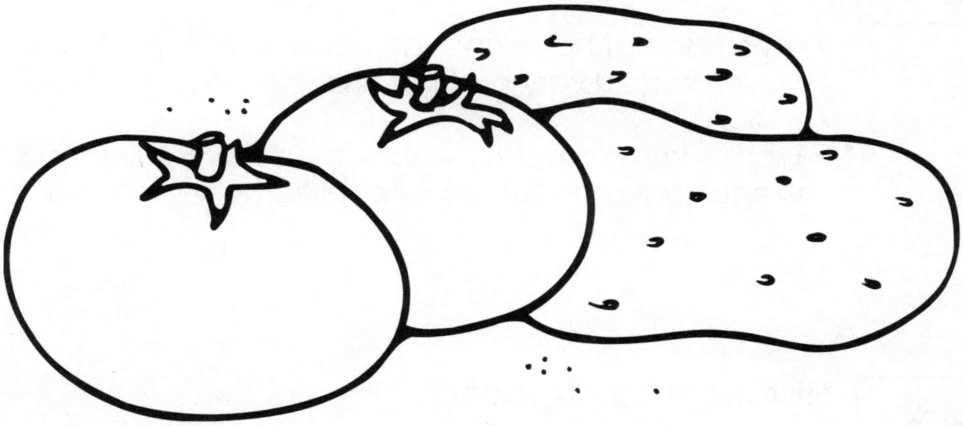

Values Education Experience

- Thomas Jefferson was a man of principle, who fought for what he believed in. Ask students what they believe in. What principles do they believe are worth sacrificing for?

Follow-Up/Homework Idea

- Invite students to talk about Thomas Jefferson and the Declaration of Independence with their families tonight.

Dictionary Day

April 14

Setting the Stage

- Begin a class tradition of writing a sentence or question on the board with an unfamiliar word in it. The unfamiliar word may be related to the daily theme or emphasis. Students need to find the definition each day.
- If you do not have enough classroom dictionaries, borrow some from your school library or other teachers, especially for today's activities.
- Construct a semantic web with facts your students know (or would like to know) about dictionaries to help you plan the day.

Historical Background

The first edition of *Webster's American Dictionary of the English Language* was published on this day in 1828.

Literary Exploration

What Do You Mean?: Story of Noah Webster by Jeri Ferris
What's in a Word? by Rosalie Moscovitch

Language Experience

- Divide students into small groups. Assign each group an unfamiliar word which they will need to look up in a dictionary. Each group writes two false, but believable, definitions of the word as well as the real definition. They mix up the definitions then join with the other groups. They attempt to stump one another. Teams take turns giving their word and the three definitions. The other groups guess the definition. Give points to each team that guesses correctly. This is a fun way to introduce the dictionary as a source for pronunciation, using sentences in context and meaning.

- Reinforce dictionary skills (using guide words, pronunciation keys and words in context).

Writing Experience

- Give students small notebooks or pages stapled together so they can make their own pocket dictionary. They label each page with a letter of the alphabet. When they discover how to spell new words, pronounce them and define them, they can add them to their dictionary. Have them also use the word in a sentence. Let them add illustrations where appropriate. See patterns for pocket dictionary on pages 95-99.

Dictionary Day

Math Experience

- Have students work in groups to count how many words on a page of a book begin with a given letter or start with a given sound.

Dictionary Day

Science/Health Experience

- Let students search the dictionary for new scientific or technological words.

- Give students a list of chemical elements. Have them look the words up in dictionaries and use the pronunciation helps to find out how to say the words.

Social Studies Experience

- Write the name of a country on an index card and a description from the dictionary on another card. Students can look up the countries and try to match them with the correct descriptions. (Example: Phoenicia—an ancient country on the eastern coast of the Mediterranean Sea.) Store the cards in a zip-close plastic bag for students to use as they finish their work.

Music/Dramatic Experience

- Play a class game of Pictionary™. Students guess a word on a certain page in the dictionary by pictorial clues they are given. Each student must give the page number and definition of the word before a point is scored.

Physical/Sensory Experience

- Challenge each student to walk across the room balancing a small pocket dictionary on the head.

Arts/Crafts Experience

- Let students make decorative book covers for their own dictionaries.

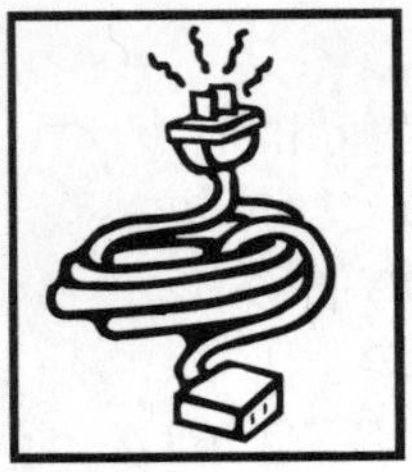

Extension Activities

- Host a Dictionary Chase! The leader chooses a word. At the signal, students race to find the word in the dictionaries and read its meaning aloud to get points for their team.

Dictionary Day

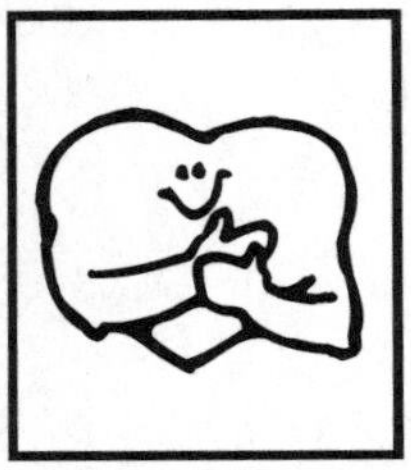

Values Education Experience

- It took Webster more than 20 years to complete his dictionary project. Discuss the value of persistence, finishing what we start. Why is this sometimes hard to do?

Dictionary Day

Follow-Up/Homework Idea

- Encourage each student to locate a dictionary in the home so it can always be found when needed.

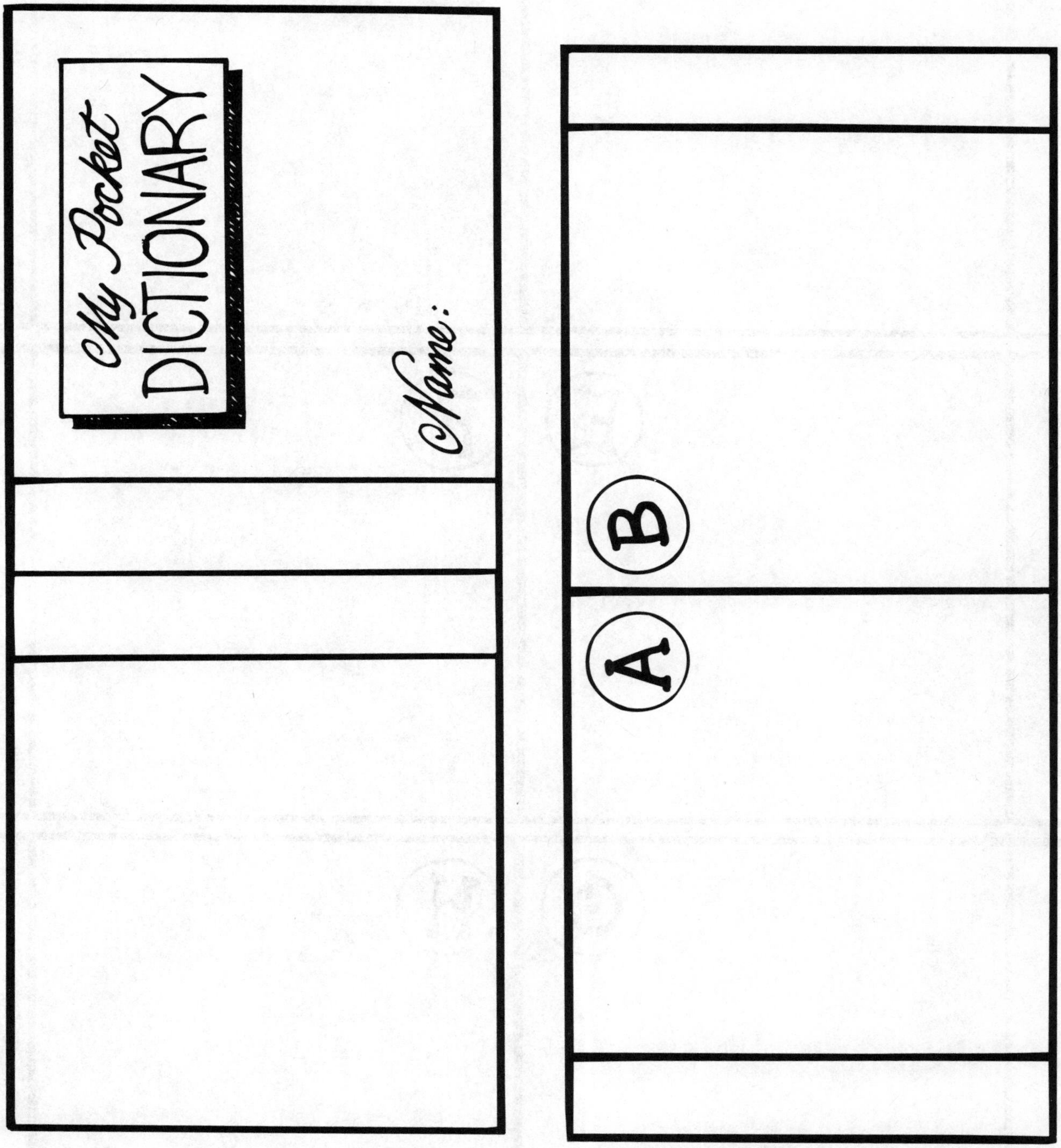
My Pocket
DICTIONARY
Name:
B
A

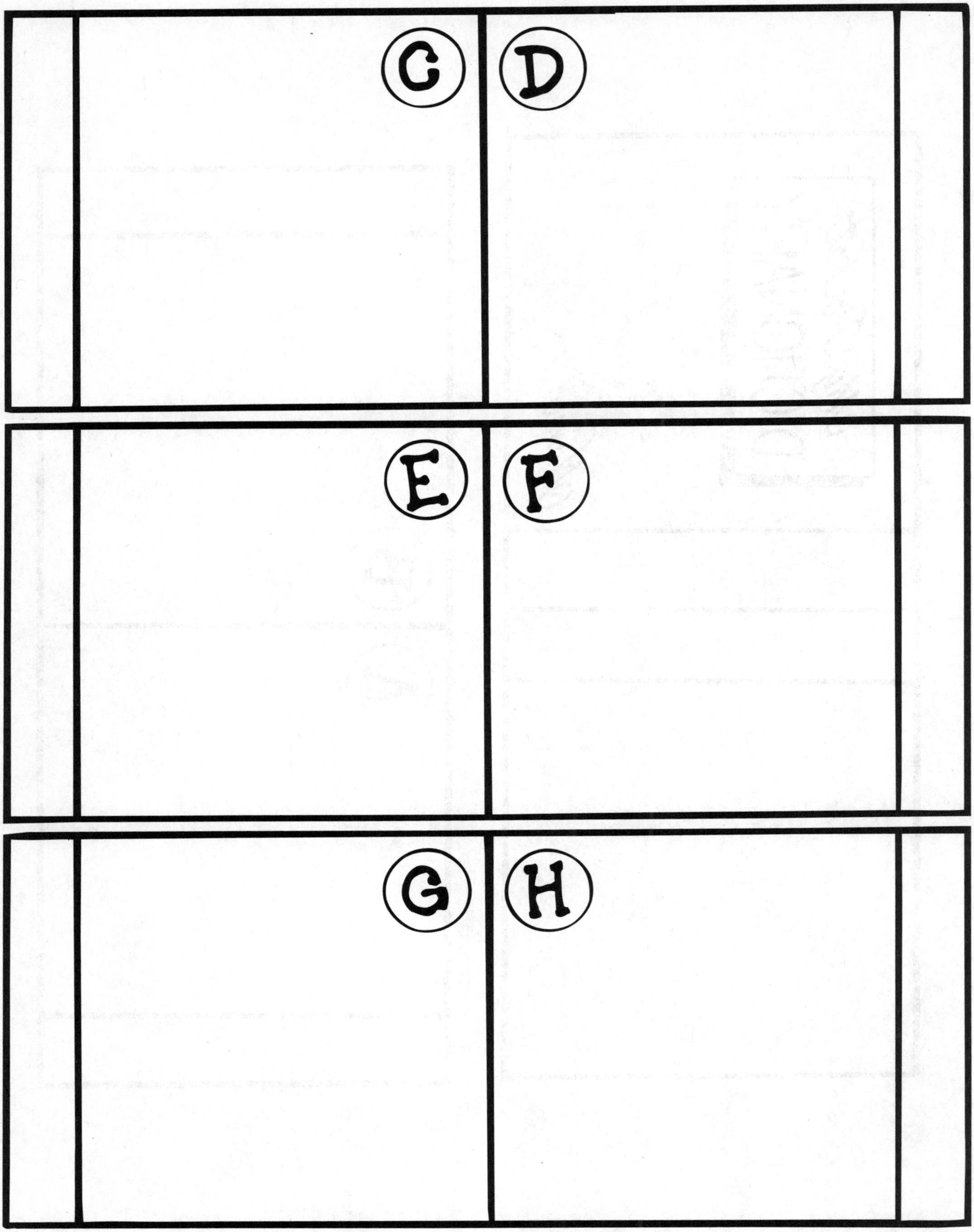
C
D
E
F
G
H

I J

K L

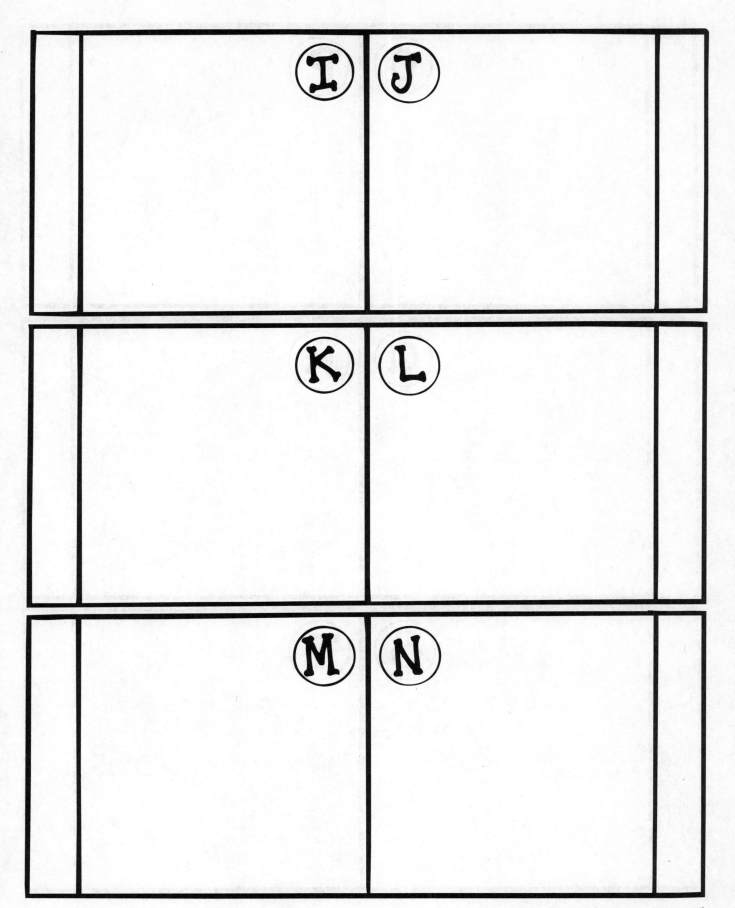

M N

O P

Q R

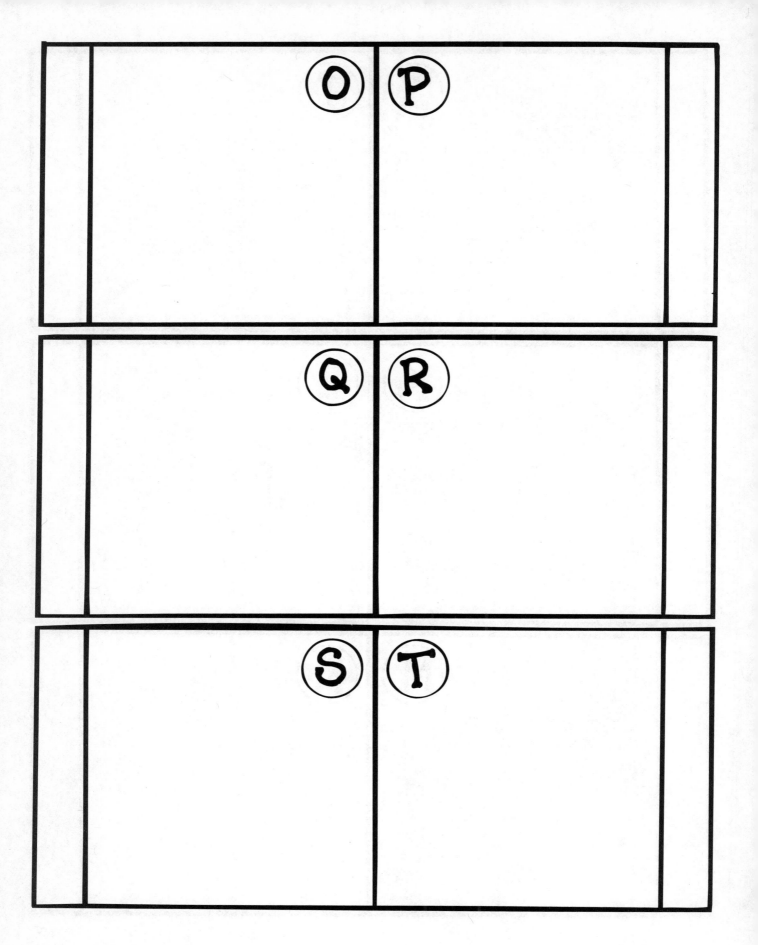

S T

U V

W X

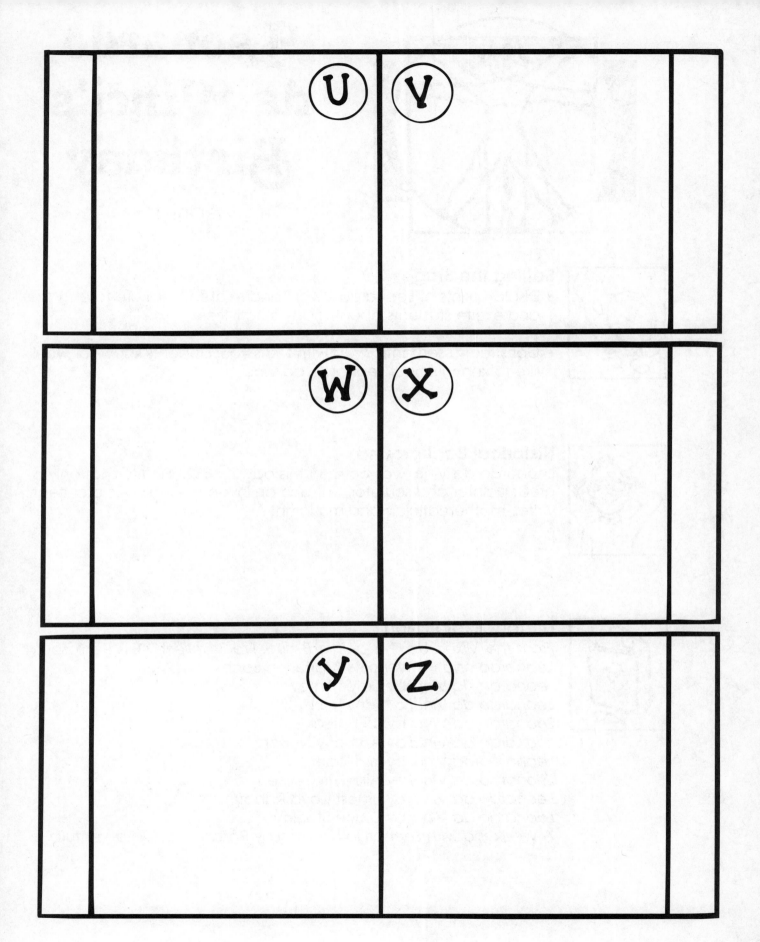

Y Z

Leonardo da Vinci's Birthday

April 15

Setting the Stage

- Display prints of Leonardo's work and related literature to engage and excite students about today's activities.
- Construct a semantic web with facts your students know (or would like to know) about Leonardo da Vinci.

Historical Background

Leonardo da Vinci was born on this day in 1452. He was not only a great painter and sculptor, but also an inventor, engineer, architect, writer, mathematician and musician!

Literary Exploration

From the Mixed-Up Files of Mrs. Basil E. Frankweiler by E.L. Konigsburg
Leonardo and His World by Marianne Sachs
Leonardo da Vinci by Peter Amey
Leonardo da Vinci by Tony Hart
Leonardo da Vinci by Ibi Lepscky
Leonardo da Vinci by Anthony Mason
Leonardo da Vinci by Iris Noble
Leonardo da Vinci by Alice Provensen
Leonardo da Vinci by Ernest Lloyd Raboff
Leonardo da Vinci by Diane Stanley
A Weekend with Leonardo da Vinci by Rosabianca Skira-Venturi

Language Experience

- How many new words can your students make using the letters in *Leonardo da Vinci*?
- Since da Vinci was Italian, your students might enjoy learning some Italian words. Try these:

    che sara, sara (kay-sa-rah, sa-rah)—what will be, will be

    arrivederci (ah-ree-vah-dayr-chee)—good-bye

    ciao (chow)—hi/so long

    scusi (skoo-zee)—excuse me

Writing Experience

- Display a picture of the Mona Lisa. Ask students why they think she is smiling. Have them write their answers. See reproducible on page 104.
- Some of Leonardo's notes about his sketches were written backwards, so they could only be read with a mirror. Give each student a hand mirror. Challenge them to write backwards messages that can only be read by another student with a mirror. See reproducible on page 105.

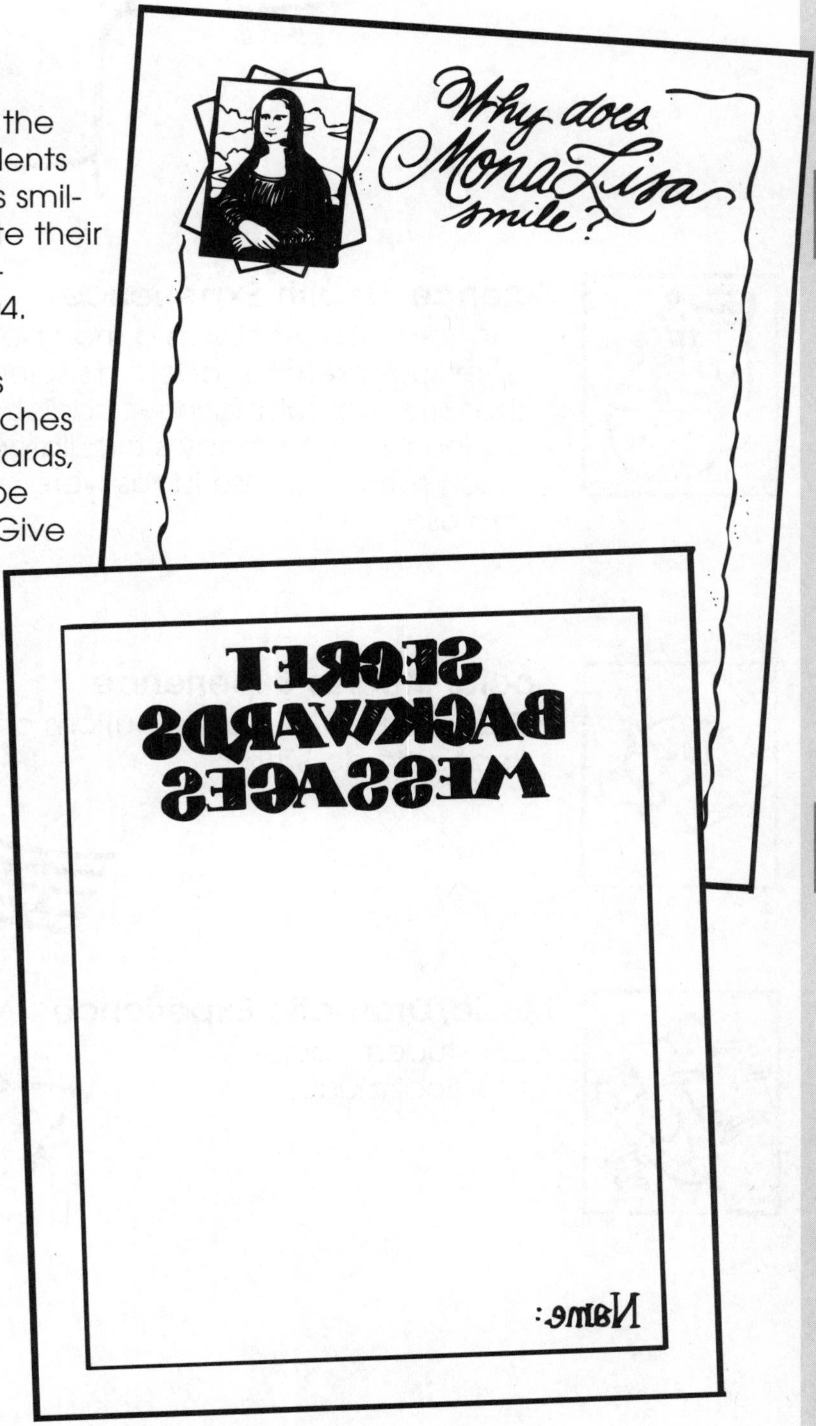
Why does Mona Lisa smile?
SECRET BACKWARDS MESSAGES
Name:

Math Experience

- Leonardo da Vinci said a person's arm span from fingertip to fingertip is about the same length as his or her height. Let students check to see if this is true for each of them. Let them measure each other's arm spans with a yardstick or rulers.

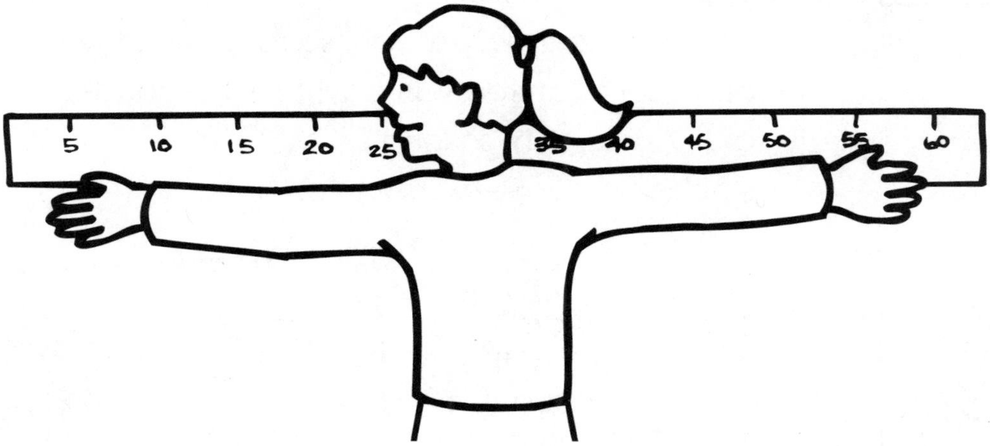

Leonardo da Vinci

Science/Health Experience

- Leonardo da Vinci was a man before his time. He made hundreds of notebook sketches about his scientific and mechanical ideas such as: the airplane, submarine, paddleboat, a self-propelled car, a clock, a cannon and the body's circulatory system. Let your students research when some of these ideas were actually accepted by others and put into use.

Social Studies Experience

- Study the life and contributions of Leonardo da Vinci.

Music/Dramatic Experience

- Let students paint to classical music.

Leonardo da Vinci

Arts/Crafts Experience

- Study Leonardo da Vinci's art style. Explore some of the patterns in his great works (such as the contrasts of light and dark or pyramid design). Challenge your students to try some of these techniques in their own masterpieces. Emery Kellen's *Leonardo da Vinci's Advice to Artists* may be a helpful resource.

Extension Activities

- Visit a local art gallery or invite an artist who specializes in oil paintings to visit your class and talk about his or her work.

Follow-Up/Homework Idea

- Leonardo was a great observer. Challenge your students to be observers on their way home today. They can make rough sketches (as Leonardo did) of something they see.

Why does Mona Lisa smile?

SECRET BACKWARDS MESSAGES

Name:

Charlie Chaplin's Birthday

April 16

Setting the Stage

- Begin the day by explaining that today the classroom will be silent (like a silent movie). Instead of talking, all communication will be written. Display a sign on the door that explains that no talking is allowed because your class is involved in a Write-a-Thon. You can communicate to students by writing on the board or individual notes. Students can write you notes, too. Everything must be written in complete sentences. Students will enjoy the novelty and fun of it all but may not be aware that they are practicing written language skills! See pattern on page 108.

Historical Background

Silent film star and comedian Charlie Chaplin was born on this day in 1889 in London, England. He made his first stage appearance at age 5 and by age 8 was touring in a musical. He came to New York City in 1910 and three years later started making silent movies in Hollywood. Chaplin made more than 60 movies in one four-year period and was one of the most popular movie stars in the world! He died in 1975.

Literary Exploration

Charlie Chaplin by Gloria Kamen

The Importance of Charlie Chaplin by Arthur Diamond

Language Experience

- Students will reinforce their language skills through written language during the all-day class Write-a-Thon.

Writing Experience

- Students can choose to write from one of the following story starters:

  I woke up one morning and could not talk . . .

  The problems that can come from talking . . . and not talking . . .

  The day the noise stopped . . .

  See reproducible on page 109.

Social Studies Experience

- Study the life of Charlie Chaplin and his contributions to the film industry.

Music/Dramatic Experience

- Let students pantomime actions like Charlie Chaplin (brushing teeth, eating corn on the cob, dressing, etc.).

Follow-Up/Homework Idea

- Challenge students to take 30 minutes at home to do something (anything) without making a single sound!

Silence
PLEASE!
Today
we are involved in a
Write-a-thon

Name:

Technology Day

April 17

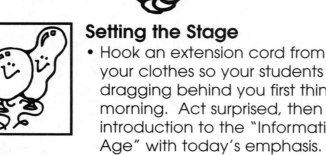

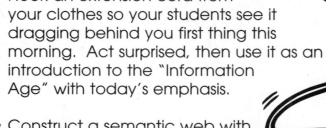

Setting the Stage

- Hook an extension cord from your clothes so your students see it dragging behind you first thing this morning. Act surprised, then use it as an introduction to the "Information Age" with today's emphasis.

- Construct a semantic web with facts your students know or would like to know about computers and technology. This will help you plan the structure of the day.

Historical Background

Since the invention of the computer, business offices (and even homes) have become technology centers with phones, faxes, computers and printers, copiers, scanners and more. Even in school, children become comfortable with the latest technology, sometimes more so than their parents.

Literary Exploration

Here Come the Robots by Joyce Milton
How Computers Work by Ian Litterick
Robots by Kate Petty
Robots and Intelligent Machines by Ian Litterick
The Story of Computers by Ian Litterick
Technology by Robin McKie

Language Experience

- Teach the basics of computer language: *software, hardware, printer, floppy disks, disk drive, monitor* and *keyboard*. Write the words on the board and have students define them if they can.

Writing Experience

- Let students practice their keyboarding skills as they type their latest writing assignment on computers.

Math Experience

- Make a mini "robot" with a box that has a slot in the back. Explain that the robot keeps changing its mind about its favorite number. It likes to work with one number for awhile, then change it. Say: "Right now its favorite number is 6. If I put a slip of paper with a 7 on it, what number will come out the slot on the other side?" (13) Review other sample problems, then let students practice with the robot. They can practice computation with unknown numbers. (If I put in this number and add or subtract this number, what number will come out?) If your students can handle the challenge, let them do missing addends.

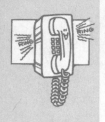

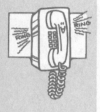

Science/Health Experience

- Study technological advances over the last century. Students can predict what advances may continue in the future. (Example: virtual reality)

Social Studies Experience

- Discuss the term *Information Revolution*. Study the history of technological inventions. Add these inventions to a class time line.

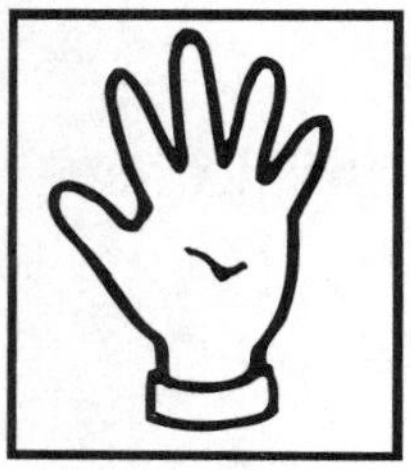

Physical/Sensory Experience

- Let students practice basic keyboarding skills on a computer. Let them also use a mouse. Ask them why a gentle touch works better on a computer than a heavy hand.

Arts/Crafts Experience

- Divide your students into cooperative groups and let them make robots from boxes, cardboard tubes, plastic tubs and lids, Styrofoam™ pieces, empty egg cartons and other craft materials. Their imaginations and creativity can run wild!

Extension Activities

⚠ Students will enjoy Edible Keyboard Mice! Serve each of them a canned pear half (body) with almond slivers for ears, a raisin nose and a thin licorice tail.

- Invite a representative from an electronics store to visit your class to talk about what's new in technology.

Follow-Up/Homework Idea

- Invite students to count how many technological appliances they have in their homes (toasters, microwaves, radios, etc.).

Paul Revere Day

April 18

Setting the Stage

- Display pictures of the Revolutionary War era and related literature around a real American flag.
- Construct a semantic web with facts your students know about America's struggle for independence. Ask them to help you make a list of questions they would like answered during the course of the day.

Historical Background

The American patriot, Paul Revere, took his "midnight" ride on this day in 1775. Leaving Boston about 10:00 p.m., he rode to Concord warning Americans of the British invasion.

Literary Exploration

American Revolutionaries by Milton Meltzer
America's Paul Revere by Esther Forbes
And Then What Happened, Paul Revere? by Jean Fritz
The Fighting Ground by Avi
Johnny Tremain by Esther Forbes
The Midnight Ride of Paul Revere by Henry Wadsworth Longfellow
Paul Revere by Lee Martin
Paul Revere: Boston Patriot by Augusta Stevenson
Paul Revere: Patriot & Craftsman by Dan Zadra, et al
A Picture Book of Paul Revere by David A. Adler

Math Experience

- Encourage your students to be "Minute Men" and "Minute Women," solving addition, subtraction or multiplication problems in a minute.

Social Studies Experience

- Study the Revolutionary War and the patriots who fought for our country's freedom.
- Have students locate Boston on a Massachusetts map. Then have them find Concord and figure out about how far Paul Revere rode that night.

Music/Dramatic Experience

- Let students role-play the Boston Tea Party or Paul Revere's ride.
- Sing the American traditional favorite, "Yankee Doodle" together.

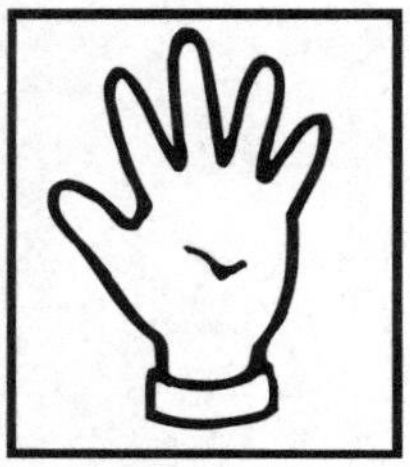

Physical/Sensory Experience

- Play "One if by Land, Two if by Sea," (like Red Light, Green Light). One student (Paul Revere) stands in a corner of the room with a flashlight and gives a signal of one flash of light or two. If students across the room see one light, they "gallop" as if on a horse. If they see two lights, they "row" as if in a boat. They continue until they reach "Paul Revere." If they hear "Paul Revere" call, "The British are coming!" they stop where they are. Anyone who moves must go back to the starting place. The first one to reach "Paul Revere" takes his or her place and the game begins again.

Arts/Crafts Experience

- Let students work together to draw a mural of the scene of Paul Revere's famous ride.

Extension Activities

⚠ Let your students make and sample "Johnnycake," a food popular in Paul Revere's time.

Johnny Cake

1 c. cornmeal
1 tsp. cream of tartar
1/2 tsp. baking soda
1/4 tsp. salt
Combine and then add:
1/4 c. honey
1 T. molasses
1 T. melted butter
1 c. milk
1 beaten egg
Put in greased 8" pan. Bake at 425°F for about 25 minutes.
Serve with homemade butter.

Follow-Up/Homework Idea

- Encourage students to go safely home "whether by land or by sea."

Bicycle Fun Day

April 19

Setting the Stage

- Display a bicycle safety helmet with bicycle-related literature.

- Construct a semantic web with words your students think of when you say "Bicycle Safety."

Historical Background

The very first known organized bike race was held outside Paris, France, on this day in 1868. The "velocipedes" was invented in 1863 in Paris, France. It was a two-wheeled machine that barely resembled today's bike, but many changes were made to it over the years until 1885 when it began to look like what we know as the bicycle. The first bicycles in America were manufactured in 1878.

Literary Exploration

Bicycle Bear by Michaela Muntean
Bicycle Bear Rides Again by Michaela Muntean
Bicycle Race by Donald Crews
Bike Factory by Harold Roth
The Bike Lesson by Stan Berenstain
D.W. Rides Again by Marc Brown
My Bike by Donna Jakob
Summer Wheels by Eve Bunting
A Tale of Two Bicycles: Safety on Your Bike by Leonard Kessler

Language Experience

- Create a Venn diagram depicting similarities and differences between traveling by bike or by car.
- Let students brainstorm words that rhyme with the word *bike*.
- Write a "bicycle for sale" newspaper ad. Include several errors in spelling, grammar and punctuation. Give each student a copy of the ad to correct. Then go over it together to check their work.

Writing Experience

- Let students put together a booklet of rules for bike safety. Have them come up with safety rules as a class. Write them on the board so students can copy them in their booklets. Fold the pattern on page 122 in fourths.

Bicycle Fun
Bicycle Fun

Science/Health Experience

- Review rules for bicycle safety, including traffic laws and turning signals.
- Discuss the value of exercising every day. What parts of the body is bicycling good for?

Music/Dramatic Experience

- Let students role-play bike safety situations.

Physical/Sensory Experience

- Set up an obstacle course for students to complete on tricycles!
- Learn bicycle hand signals.

- Let students lie on their backs, put their feet in the air and do "bicycling" for exercise.
- Demonstrate with a real bike how to care for it and keep it in good working order. (Check brakes, headlights, tire air pressure, clean and lubricate the chain, apply reflector tape and make sure screws and bolts are fastened securely.)

Arts/Crafts Experience

- Let students decorate their bicycles (or tricycles) with streamers and ribbons. Then let them ride in a parade around the school.

- Have students make safety posters urging everyone to practice safety on their bicycles. (Wagon wheel pasta makes great miniature bicycle wheels.)

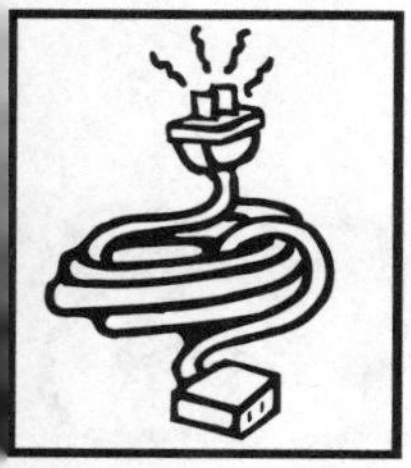

Extension Activities

- Ask other teachers if they would like to join your class in a Bicycle Safety Rodeo. Local police departments are happy to help with safety programs and send officers to help students with safety-related activities.

TRAFFIC LIGHTS
ARE FOR BIKES TOO!

Follow-Up/Homework Idea

- Encourage students to have a good time on their bikes and practice safety rules as they ride in their neighborhoods.

Caring for my BICYCLE.....

BICYCLE SAFETY RULES

Train Day

April 20

Setting the Stage

- Display a miniature train around train-related literature. Wear a conductor's cap and striped overalls to greet your students.

- Display your students' best work surrounded by trains with the caption: "You're on the Right Track!"

- Use a train theme to encourage independent reading. Display a train engine on one wall of the room. Encourage students to read books so they can get train cars with their names and the book name on the wall. See train patterns on pages 128-130.

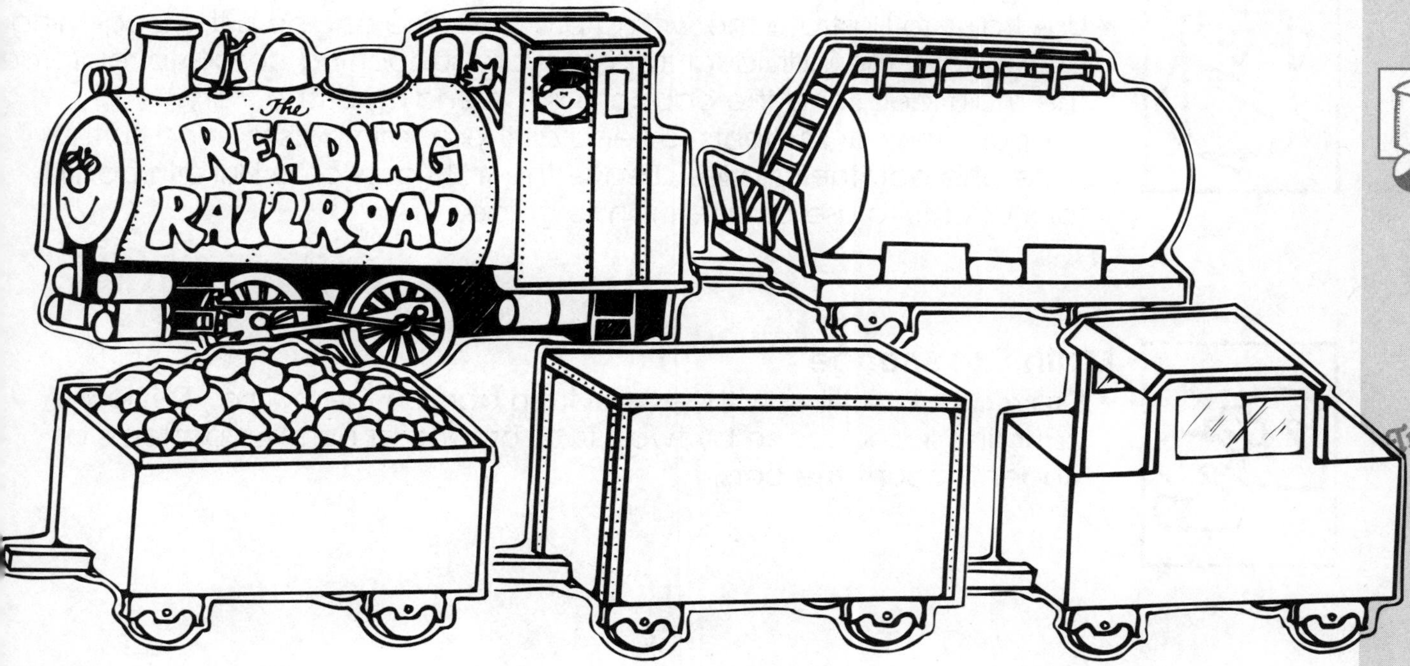

Literary Exploration

The Everyday Train by Amy Ehrlich
Hey, Get off Our Train by John Burningham
If I Drove a Train by Miriam Young
Inside a Freight Train by Ellen Johnston McHenry
Inside Freight Train by Donald Crews
The Last Train by Kim Lewis
The Little Train by Judy Hindley
The Little Train by Lois Lenski
Short Train, Long Train by Frank Asch
Steam Train Ride by Evelyn Clarke Mott
The Train by David M. McPhail
The Train by Robert Welber
The Train Ride by June Crebbin
Train Ride by John Steptoe
Train Song by Diane Siebert
There's a Train Going by My Window by Wendy Kesselman

Language Experience

- Let your students brainstorm words that have the long "a" sound (ai) as in *train*.
- Let students brainstorm train "language" with words such as: *passenger, all aboard, conductor, engineer*, etc. (Some words such as *choo-choo* are still used though they're out of date.)

Writing Experience

- Use trains to illustrate the writing process. The engine is the beginning of the story, the individual train cars are supporting details to reinforce the main idea, and the caboose is the ending of the story. Encourage your students to keep all these train cars in mind as they write and edit their stories. Leave the train cars on a bulletin board for students to use as a reference guide.

Math Experience

- Draw a train outline with several train cars on the board. Review counting in sequence by twos, fives or tens, or number patterns as students count the cars.

Science/Health Experience

- Study how modern trains work.
- Study how steam trains work. Do some experiments with steam.

Social Studies Experience

- Have students research how trains have evolved over the years. Let them share their findings with the rest of the class.

Music/Dramatic Experience

- Sing the song "I've Been Working on the Railroad."

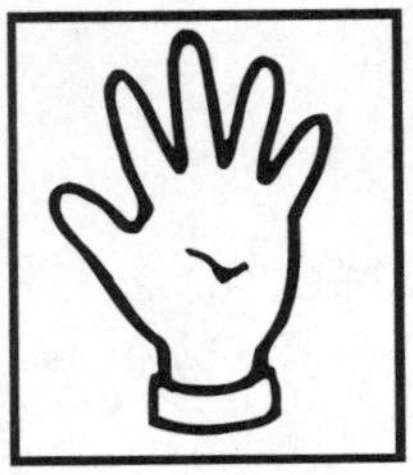

Physical/Sensory Experience

- Play Follow the Conductor, Hang on Caboose! Students form a line and put their hands on the waist of the person in front of them. The conductor shouts, "Toot! Toot," and the first person in line (the "engine") runs around the room or track with the others following.

- Students will enjoy the Train Track Game. Lay down sheets of black construction paper (two sets) like "tracks" across the floor. Two teams compete against each other. They all stand on the "tracks." The last person on each team picks up his train track, runs to the front of the line, lays it down and stands on it. The last person repeats this process. When all the tracks are on the other side of the playing area and the original first person is at the head of the line again, the relay is over.

Arts/Crafts Experience

- Provide large cardboard boxes to represent train cars. Students can paint and decorate them and role-play train trips.

Arts/Crafts Experience continued

- Let students make conductor's signal lanterns by folding a 9" x 12" piece of construction paper lengthwise. On the fold, they cut slits about an inch apart across the paper to about one inch from the edge. They unfold the paper then overlap the uncut edges and staple them together. A paper handle can be glued or stapled to the top.

- Each student can make a train conductor's hat by trimming about 6" from the top of a white paper lunch bag. They can draw thin black stripes around it and turn it upside down to wear.

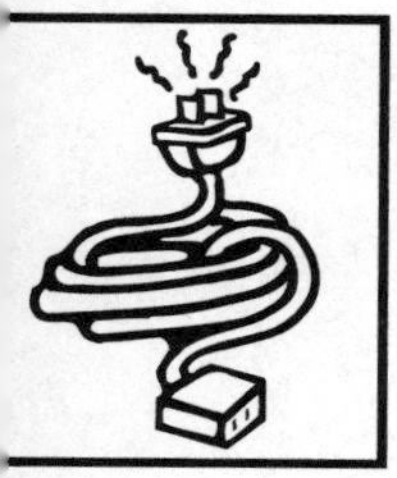

Extension Activities

⚠ Let students make Edible Trains by sticking graham crackers together with frosting. Round peppermint candies can be added for wheels and a chocolate candy kiss for a smokestack.

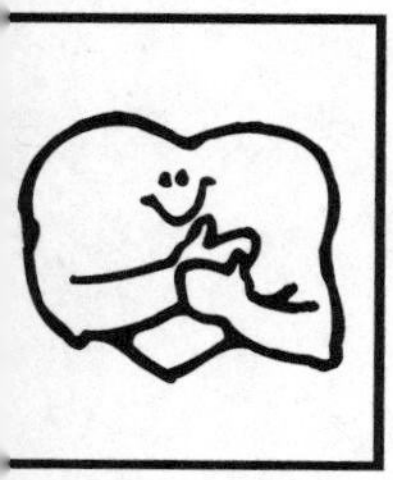

Values Education Experience

- Remember the story *The Little Engine That Could*? Discuss the phrase, "I know I can, I know I can" to encourage your students to believe in themselves and their ability to make their dreams come true.

Follow-Up/Homework Idea

- Invite students to tell their families what they learned about trains today.

The
READING
RAILROAD

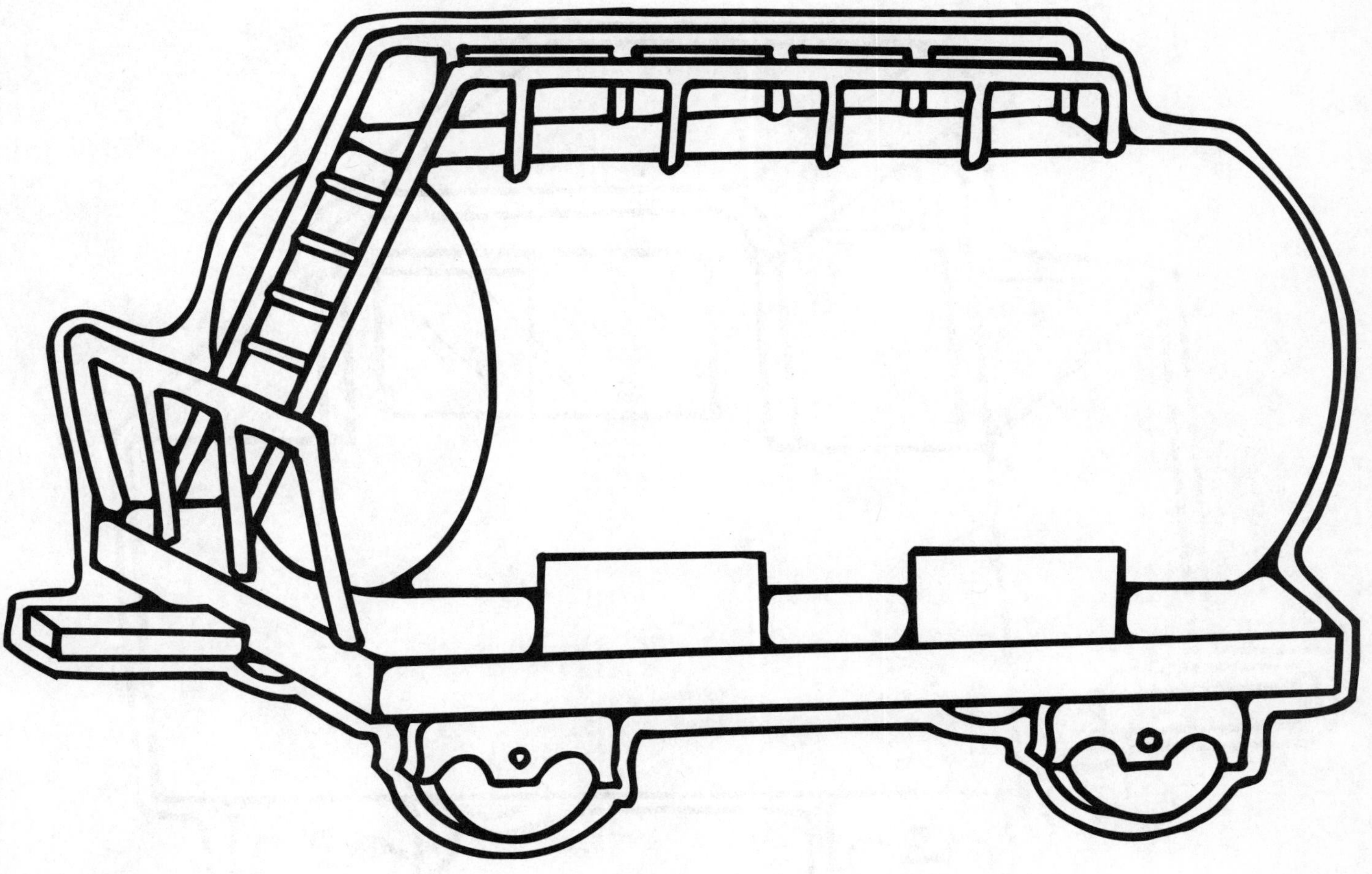

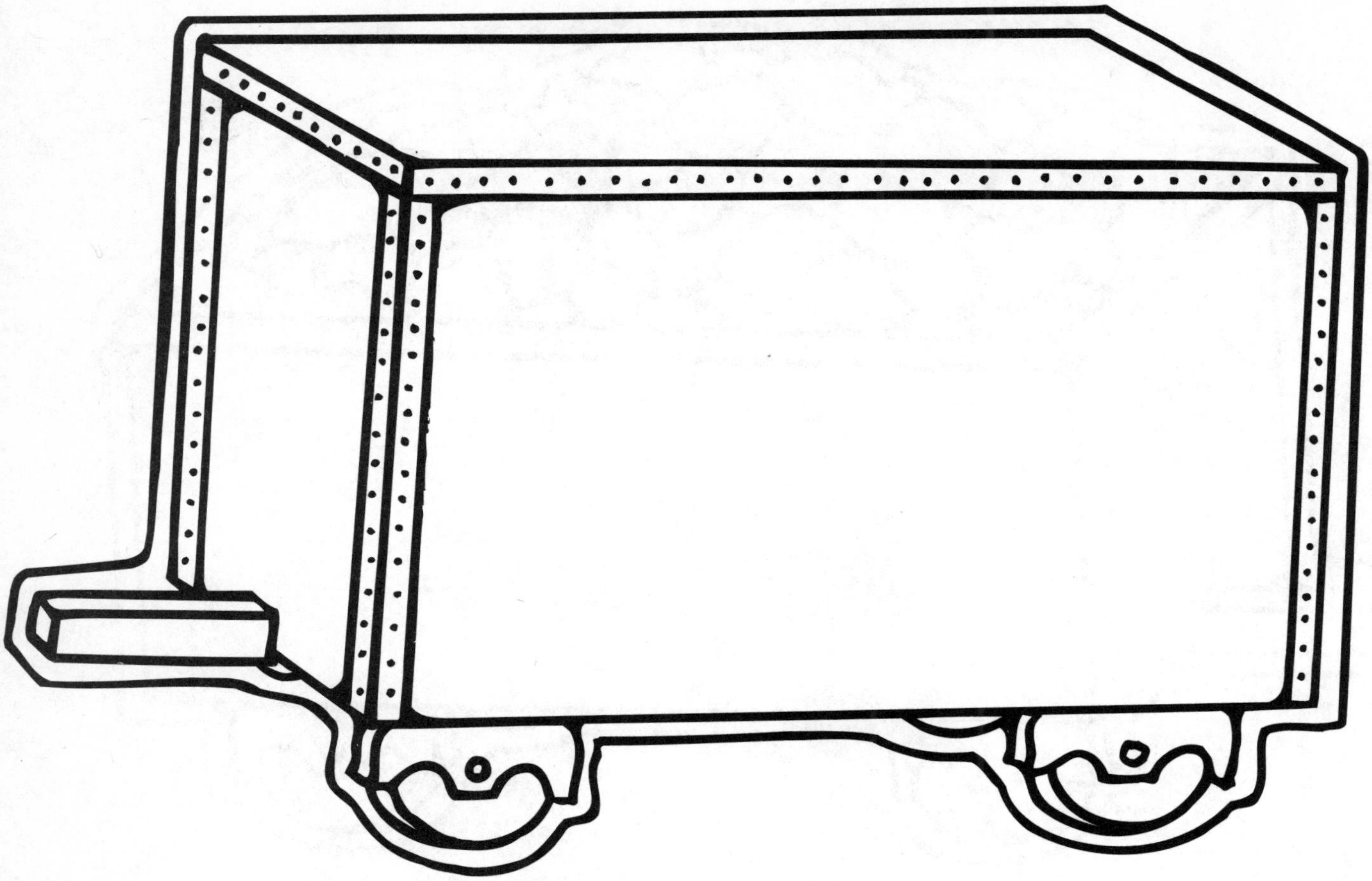

Hug a Tree Day

April 21

Setting the Stage

- Display pictures of trees and tree by-products around tree-related literature.

- Construct a semantic web with facts your students know about trees. Ask them to list questions about trees they would like answered.

Historical Background

Julius Sterling Morton, a journalist and politician in Nebraska, believed his state needed more trees. He planted many trees on his own farm and urged his neighbors to do the same. He convinced Nebraska leaders to set a day aside especially for planting trees. They called it Arbor Day and one million trees were planted that day in 1872. In the year that followed, other states picked up the idea and millions of trees were planted all across America.

Literary Exploration

All About Trees by Jane Dickinson
Arbor Day by Diane L. Burns
Child's Book of Trees by Valerie Swenson
Tree (Eyewitness Books) by David Burnie
The Giving Tree by Shel Silverstein
Look Inside a Tree by Gina Ingoglia
The Lorax by Dr. Seuss
Mr. Tamarin's Trees by Kathryn Ernst
The Old Man Who Made Trees Blossom by Hanasaka JiJii
Once There Was a Tree by Natalia Romanova
Red Leaf, Yellow Leaf by Lois Ehlert
Someday a Tree by Eve Bunting
A Tree in the Wood: An Old Nursery Song by Christopher Manson
A Tree Is Nice by Janice May Udry
Trees by Illa Podendorf
Trees and Forests by Galliamard Jeunesse
The Tremendous Tree Book by Barbara Brenner and May Garelick

Language Experience

- As a class, brainstorm reasons trees are useful (providing oxygen and shade, furniture, paper, homes for animals, etc.).

- Have students think of words that have the "ee" sound as in *tree*. Print the words on the board.

Writing Experience

- Have students write about why we need trees. Let them write on a tree shape. See reproducible on page 136.

Math Experience

- Take students outside to measure around the trunks of various trees with pieces of string. Then they measure the strings and make a note of each tree and its trunk size on a list. Back in the classroom they can add the data to a class graph.

Science/Health Experience

- Study the different varieties of trees and how they grow. Which trees are evergreens? Which are deciduous?

- Take students outside on a leaf hunt. Have them collect leaves from a variety of trees, then look them up to identify them.

Hug a Tree

Hug a Tree

Social Studies Experience

- Review mapping skills by letting your students map out where the trees are located in your school yard.

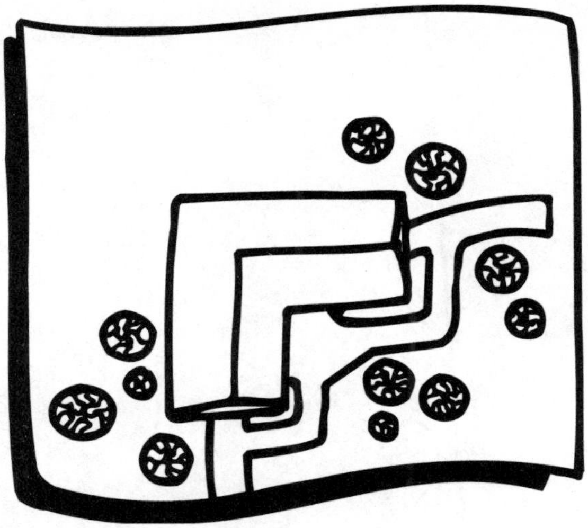

Music/Dramatic Experience

- Sing "A Tree in the Wood: An Old Nursery Song" by Christopher Manson.
- Read aloud the poem "Trees" by Joyce Kilmer.

Physical/Sensory Experience

- Let students make leaf rubbings; but also make trunk rubbings so they can see and feel the unique textures of tree trunks.

- Take students outside and let them each hug a tree!

Arts/Crafts Experience

- Let students draw a forest full of trees using tempera paints.
- Students can design their "dream" tree houses for their backyards.

Extension Activities

- Let your class plant a tree at your school. (Sometimes nurseries or greenhouses are willing to donate small trees to a worthy cause.)

⚠ Students can eat Edible Trees (broccoli)! They can dip them in cheese or vegetable dip to make them a little more "user friendly"!

- Invite a member of the Forest Service to visit your class and talk about his or her work.

Values Education Experience

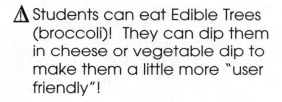

- Discuss how students can show their appreciation for trees by taking care of them.

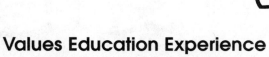

Follow-Up/Homework Idea

- Invite your students to count the trees they see on their way home.

Earth Day

April 22

Setting the Stage

- Display all kinds of recyclable trash products (plastics, aluminum, glass, paper) around a world globe or a large picture of the Earth with the caption: "What on EARTH are we doing?"

- Let each student write a way to help save the Earth and write it on an adhesive bandage. (Examples: recycle, conserve water, save paper, turn out lights after use, reuse, car pool and avoid littering) Display a large picture of the Earth. Let students place their bandages on it with the caption: "We Can All Do Our Part to Help Heal the Earth."

Setting the Stage continued

- Construct a semantic web with facts your students know about conserving the Earth's resources. Then list their questions they would like answered today.

Historical Background

In 1963 President John Kennedy went on an 11-state conservation tour to get the American people to think about the natural environment. But it wasn't until April 22, 1970, that the first Earth Day was held. Since then, people have been more concerned about solving Earth's environmental problems. Earth Day is now an annual event throughout the United States on April 22.

Literary Exploration

Brother Eagle, Sister Sky: A Message from Chief Seattle by Susan Jeffers
Cartons, Cans, and Orange Peels: Where Does Your Garbage Go? by Joanna Foster
Celebrating Earth Day by Robert Gardner
Crocodile Smile: 10 Songs of the Earth as the Animals See It by Sarah Weeks
Dinosaurs to the Rescue: A Guide to Protecting Our Planet by Laurie Krasny Brown and Marc Brown
Earth by Seymour Simon
The Earth by Caroline Arnold
The Earth Is Painted Green by Barbara Brenner
50 Simple Things Kids Can Do to Save the Earth by John Javna
For the Love of Our Earth by P.K. Halinan
Going Green: A Kid's Handbook to Saving the Planet by John Elkington
The Great Kapok Tree by Lynne Cherry
How Green Are You? by David Bellamy
Just a Dream by Chris Van Allsburg
The Magic School Bus Gets Eaten: A Book About Food Chains by JoAnna Cole
Mrs. Fish, Ape, and Me, the Dump Queen by Norma Fox Mazer
My First Green Book by Angela Wilkes
One Earth, a Multitude of Creatures by Peter and Connie Roop
Recycle! A Handbook for Kids by Gail Gibbons
Rescue Mission: Planet Earth by Peace Child International
Save the Earth by Consumer Guide
Save the Earth by Lina Longo Hirsch
The Wartville Wizard by Don Madden
Tommorrow's Earth: A Squeaky-Green Guide by David Bellamy
Where Does the Garbage Go? by Paul Showers
World Water Watch by Michelle Koch

Language Experience

- Brainstorm possible cleanup, beautification and recycling projects. List them on the board and have students put them in alphabetical order. Plan to do at least one of the projects.

CLEAN
UP
AMERICA

Writing Experience

- Have students write about how we can all pitch in together to save our planet and make it a better place to live. See reproducible on page 142.

Name:
How can we
PITCH IN
to save our planet?

Science/Health Experience

- Today is a perfect day to begin a science unit on ecosystems (our interdependence upon each other) and how we can conserve our Earth's resources.

- Let students get a firsthand look at air pollution! Students spread a thin layer of petroleum jelly on a piece of wax paper. They can add a craft stick "frame" to add stability. Let students poke a hole with a hole punch in a corner of the wax paper. Then they thread string through the hole so that it can be hung from a tree branch. Let students observe and make notations as to the pollution buildup after a few days.

Music/Dramatic Experience

- Learn a few songs from *Recycled Songs* by Don Cooper.

- Challenge student pairs to write and perform raps about the environment and how we can protect it.

Physical/Sensory Experience

- Let students draw flowers and signs that say *City Park, No Littering, Obey the Law* and *Please Don't Pick the Flowers.* Scatter the pictures and signs around the room on the floor. Stick a wide strip of green tape on the floor between the signs and pictures. Let students read the signs as they try to walk on the line without losing their balance. Reinforce the idea of obeying the laws to protect and keep our world beautiful.

Arts/Crafts Experience

- Let students make posters urging others to help save the Earth. Get permission to mount the posters around the school.
- Have students experiment with water and oil-based paints, making observations about how oil spills effect bodies of water.
- Give each student a moist coffee filter. They dab "earth" watercolors (brown and green) with a cotton swab on the filter to indicate land and paint blue for the "oceans" surrounding the land areas. Glue these world paintings against a dark blue or black background and put them on a bulletin board.

Extension Activities

- Create a "Little Monster" at your school. Trace the outline of a "monster" on a large piece of butcher paper, then lay it on the floor. Supervise a trash pick up on the school grounds making sure students avoid any unsafe or unsavory items. Glue the trash on the monster shape. Label it, *Our Little Monster*. Have students take the monster to the principal's office as a gift.

Name:
How can we
PITCH IN
to save our planet?

William Shakespeare's Birthday

April 23

Setting the Stage

- "To be or not to be, that is the question!" Today, your students will learn about the world of plays and acting. Display masks, props and acting paraphernalia around literature about putting on plays or books about William Shakespeare.

- Construct a semantic web with facts your students know and understand about putting on a play. Ask them to list questions they would like answered.

Historical Background

The English playwright and poet, William Shakespeare, was born on this day in 1564. His works have been published and translated into more languages than any other book except the Bible.

Literary Exploration

Bard of Avon: The Story of William Shakespeare by Diane Stanley
Everyday Plays for Boys and Girls by Helen Louise Miller
First Plays for Children by Helen Louise Miller
Round the World Plays for Young People by Paul T. Nolan
Shakespeare for Children by Cass Foster
William Shakespeare by Ibi Lepscky
William Shakespeare by Dorothy Turner
William Shakespeare and His Plays by Charles Haines

Language Experience

- Review the basics of putting on plays and writing scripts. Don't forget setting, characters, introduction, plot, exciting action or drama and a conclusion.

- Challenge your students to each memorize a quote from Shakespeare. They can also perform choral readings such as his famous words: "To thine own self be true, and it must follow, as the night the day, thou cans't be false to any man."

- Let students brainstorm words that have the "ay" sound as in *play*.

Writing Experience

- Divide students into cooperative groups to write short imaginative plays or rewrite stories already written into play scripts.
- Challenge students to rewrite some of Shakespeare's words in their own words.

Social Studies Experience

- Study the life and contributions of William Shakespeare. Look on a map to find his birthplace.
- Drama is a part of all cultures. Review *Round the World Plays for Young People* by Paul T. Nolan to see how plays around the world are alike and how they differ.

Music/Dramatic Experience

- Let students catch the "acting bug." Dramatic play is basic to children's growth and development. It helps them to translate the adult world to a level that they can understand and control, develop a healthy self-image, practice communication, develop expression and have vicarious experiences that transcend their normal, everyday worlds. Divide students into groups and let them perform plays that they have written or dramatize favorite books.

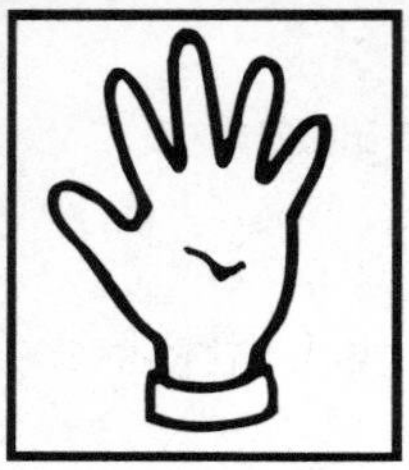

Physical/Sensory Experience

- Let students pantomime everyday activities such as: playing in the school orchestra, holding something hot, inflating a balloon that pops or eating ice cream.

Arts/Crafts Experience

- Let students draw scenery and make props for their plays.

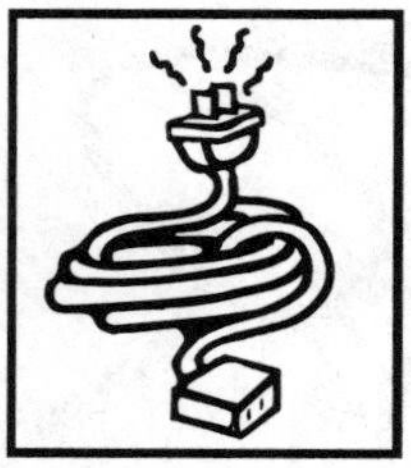

Extension Activities

- Take your class to visit a local playhouse or watch a nearby high school play together.

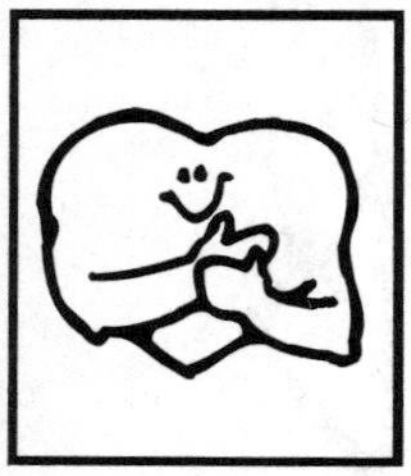

Values Education Experience

- Discuss what Shakespeare meant in his play *Hamlet* when he said, "To thine ownself be true."

Follow-Up/Homework Idea

- Challenge your students to perform plays with brothers and sisters or friends at home.

Newspaper Day

April 24

Setting the Stage

- Some newspaper offices donate free newspapers for a worthy cause. Request some for your class activities today. Handling newspaper can be very messy because of the black newsprint, so have moist paper towels to clean students' hands.
- Display a map of the world on a bulletin board. Have students cut out newspaper articles about events around the world and bring them to class. Tack the articles on the board with a piece of string leading from each one to its location on the world map. Add the caption: "What in the WORLD is going on?" A scalloped newspaper edge makes a nice border around the bulletin board.

Newspaper Day

Setting the Stage continued

- Have students draw pictures of people sitting on a park bench. Display these on a bulletin board. Glue real newspaper in the people's hands with the caption: "Keep Informed of Current Events."

- Construct a semantic web with facts your students know about newspapers and the newspaper business. Then list their questions to be answered today.

Historical Background

The first American newspaper, *The Boston News-Letter,* was published on this day in 1704. It was printed on both sides of a single sheet of paper once a week.

Literary Exploration

Behind the Newspaper Scene by D. X. Fenton
Deadline: From News to Newspaper by Gail Gibbons
Henry and the Paper Route by Beverly Cleary
Hot Off the Press! A Day at the Daily News by Margaret Miller
Newspaper Theatre by Alice Morin
What It's Like to Be a Newspaper Reporter by Janet Craig

Language Experience

- Take a newspaper apart and categorize the various sections that make up a typical newspaper (world and local news, weather, sports, entertainment, classifieds, business advertisements and an advice column). Then discuss what kinds of articles fit under those categories. Perhaps your class would be interested in making a class newspaper (using those same article ideas). Decide who will be responsible for what jobs: editors, reporters, columnists, graphic artists and cartoonists.

- Let students find five unfamiliar words in the newspaper and look up their meanings in the dictionary. Then let them share their new words and meanings with the class.

- Review comprehension skills by having students read an article and orally (or through writing) explain what the article is about in their own words.

Writing Experience

- Students can cut out the headlines of newspaper stories and make up stories to go with them. See reproducible on page 153.

- Challenge students to write their own newspaper headlines for things that have happened this week in school.

Newspaper Day

Writing Experience continued

- Students can cut out newspaper photos and captions and mount them on paper. Then they can write dialogue for the people or items in the photo. See speech balloon patterns on page 154.

Math Experience

- Brainstorm newspaper titles for a classroom newspaper. Then take a vote, tally the votes and make a bar graph of the results.

Science/Health Experience

- Let students cut out science or health-related articles in the newspaper to share with the rest of the class.

- Hand out newspapers and have students search for stories or articles on science- and health-related topics (medical topics, space, weather, etc.). Let each student read an article aloud.

Social Studies Experience

- Conduct a discussion about news of events around the world from the newspaper.
- Have students see how many different states or countries they can find mentioned in the newspaper.

Music/Dramatic Experience

- Let your students "interview" schoolmates for class newspaper articles.
- Use some of the ideas or suggestions from *Newspaper Theatre* by Alice Morin.

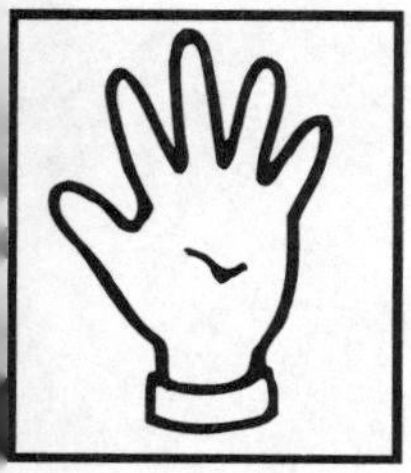

Physical/Sensory Experience

- Involve students in a newspaper relay. Divide them into relay teams. Give each student two sheets of newspaper to lay down, step on one, then lay the other down, step on it and so on. The first team that gets to the finish line, stepping only on the newspaper, wins!

- Have a newspaper scavenger hunt. Students can work in pairs or individually to find certain things in the newspaper (vowel teams, a city in Europe, a four-digit number, three compound words, "oi" and "oy" diphthongs, etc.).

Arts/Crafts Experience

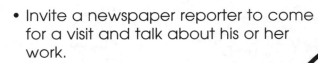

- Let students make papier-mâché figures or sculptures using newspaper.

Extension Activities

- Take a class field trip to a newspaper office to see how a newspaper progresses from ideas in someone's head to printed pages.
- Invite a newspaper reporter to come for a visit and talk about his or her work.
- Ask someone, such as an older student, who has a paper route to come and explain how he or she gets newspapers to customers.

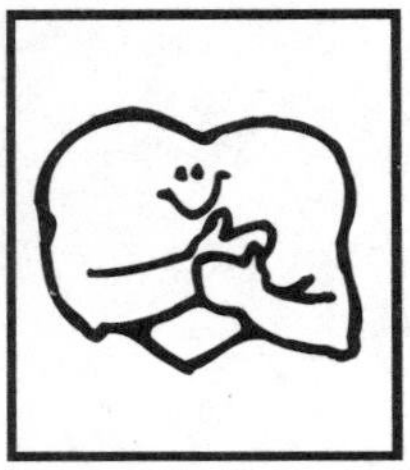

Values Education Experience

- Discuss the responsibilities the editors and reporters of a newspaper have to write and publish the truth. Talk about how each of us is also responsible for telling the truth.

Follow-Up/Homework Idea

- Encourage students to read a newspaper at home tonight.

HEADLINES

License Plate Day

April 25

Setting the Stage

- Display old license plates around a toy car. Check with a police compound or the Department of Motor Vehicles for used license plates you can have.

- Explain that today students will get their "Learner's Permits" which will enable them to take part in all activities. If there is an infraction (just as in driving), students might have their Learner's Permits revoked for a period of time and have to do "community service" (special assignments in class). See patterns on page 159.

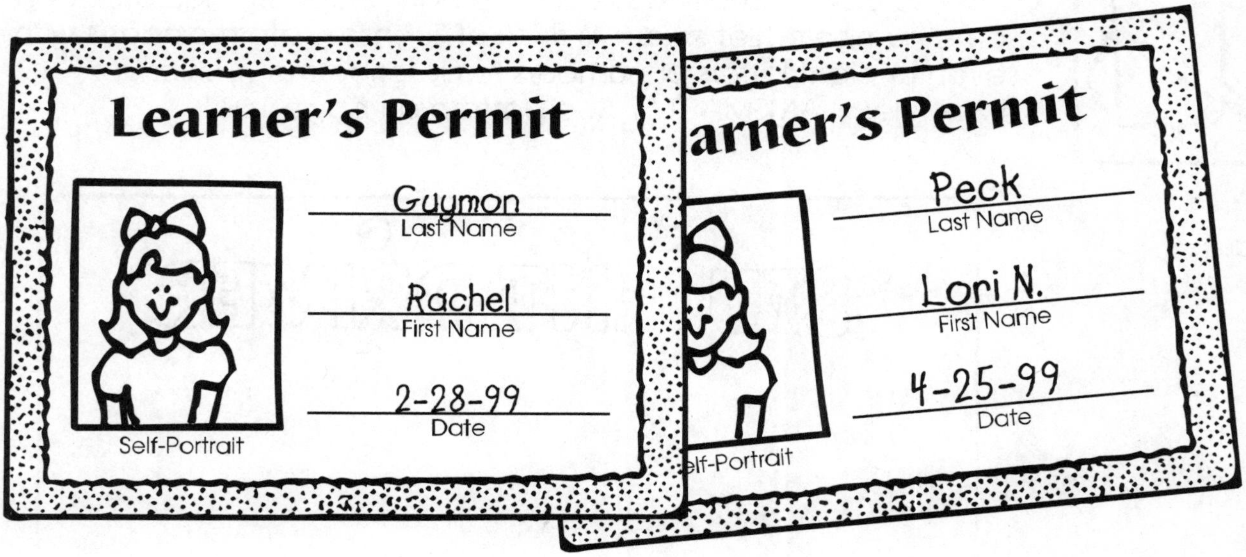

- Construct a semantic web with facts your students know about license plates. Let them think of questions they would like answered throughout the day.

Historical Background
License plates were required for the first time on automobiles in America on this day in 1901. The new requirement began in New York where they charged one dollar for each license plate.

Literary Exploration
License Plate Book by Thomson Murray
The Way Cool License Plate Book by Leonard Wise

Language Experience
- Involve your students in license plate pneumonics such as, "LUVTOLRN."
- Let students brainstorm as many words as they can that rhyme with, *plate*.

Writing Experience
- License plates usually have a state name, county indicator icon and some numbers. Let students think of license plate messages with seven or eight letters or numbers to describe themselves. (Example: "IAMSMART.") See pattern on page 160.

Math Experience

- If possible and safe, take your students out to the faculty parking lot. Let them add up the numbers on various license plates. You may want to assign a number to each letter (A = 7, B = 12, C = 10, etc.). Tell them to find license plates that add up to 10 or 16. Have them take notes so they can add the information to a bar graph when they return to the room.

- Let students measure the area and perimeter of some old license plates.

Social Studies Experience

- For a self-esteem builder, ask students to make customized license plates with their names in bold letters, then ask classmates for positive descriptive words about themselves. The words can be written in small letters around the license plates for borders. Have students display their license plates on their desks for name tags. See pattern on page 158.

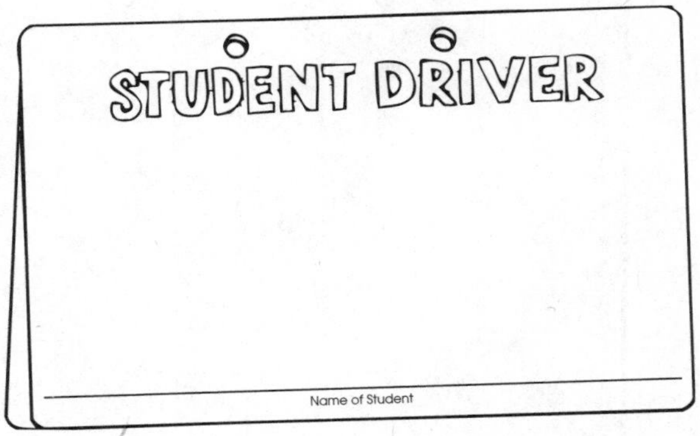

Physical/Sensory Experience

- Play License Plate Bingo! Students can fill in states on their Bingo cards as you mention them, watching for a horizontal, vertical or diagonal match. See patterns on page 161.

Arts/Crafts Experience

- Let students design their own personalized license plates with symbols and colorful borders. The plates should say something about the students.

Follow-Up/Homework Idea

- Ask students to ask their parents about when they first learned to drive.

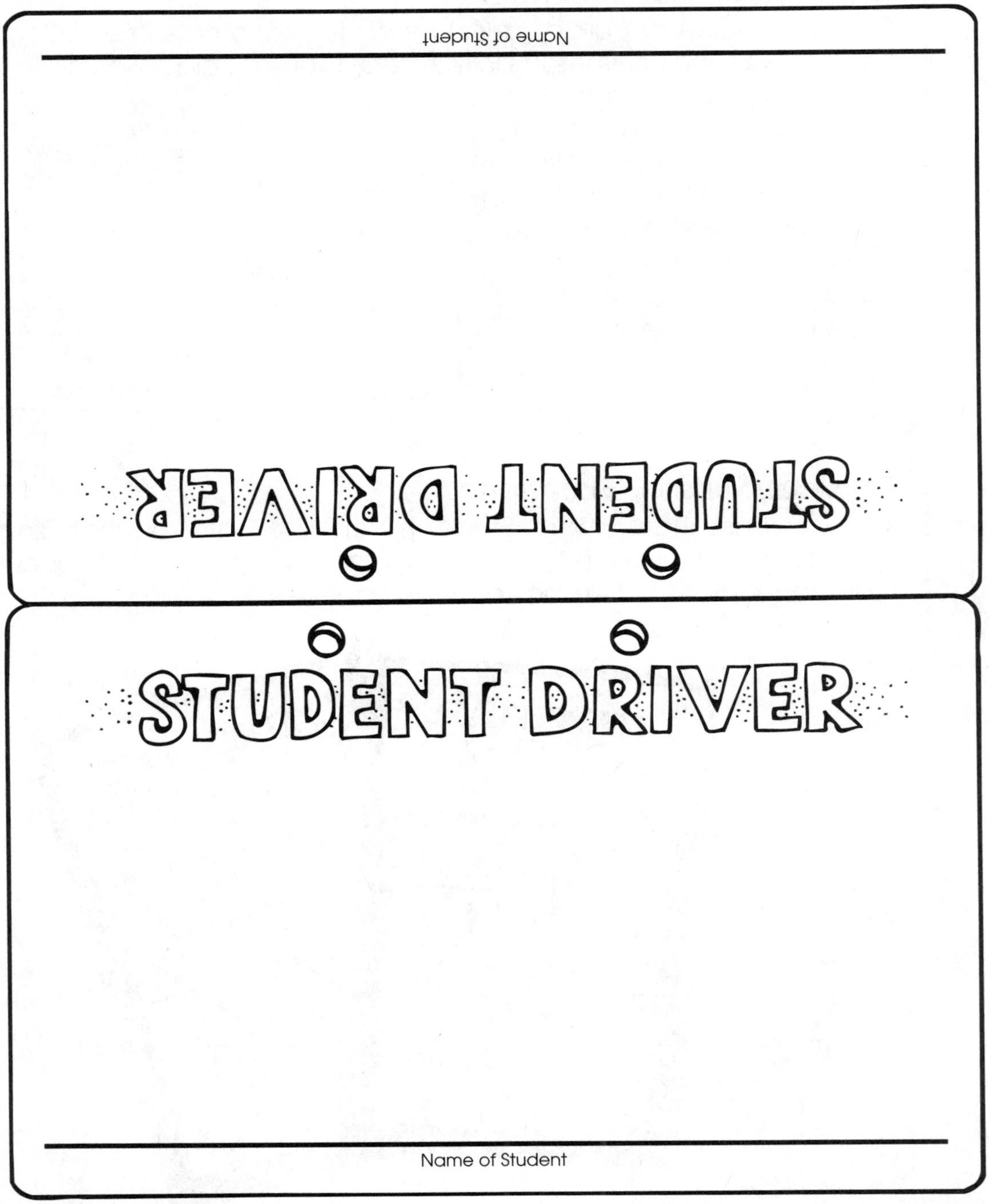

Learner's Permit

Self-Portrait

Last Name

First Name

Date

Learner's Permit

Self-Portrait

Last Name

First Name

Date

Learner's Permit

Self-Portrait

Last Name

First Name

Date

Learner's Permit

Self-Portrait

Last Name

First Name

Date

STUDENT DRIVER

____

Name of Student

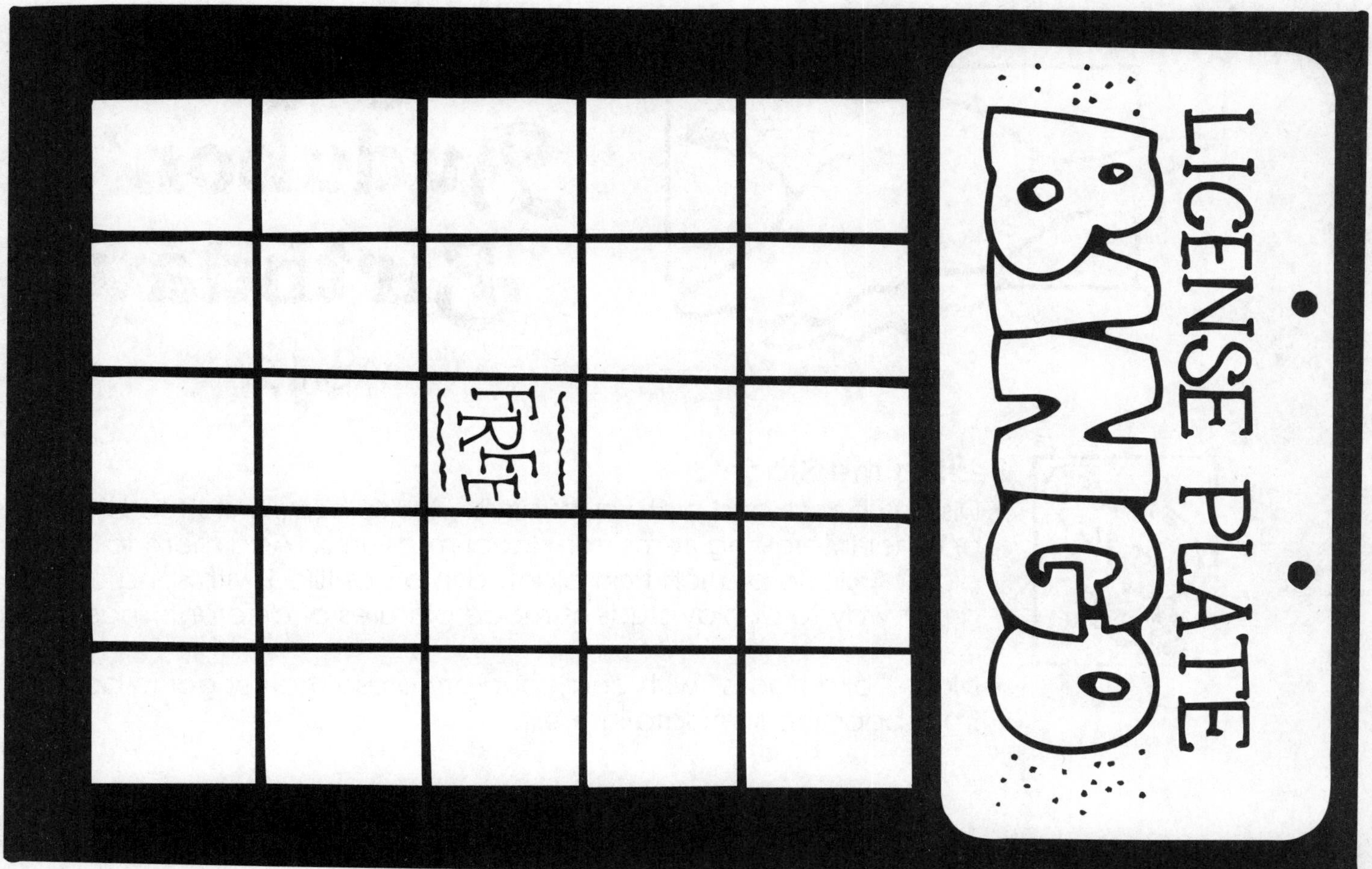
LICENSE PLATE
BINGO
FREE

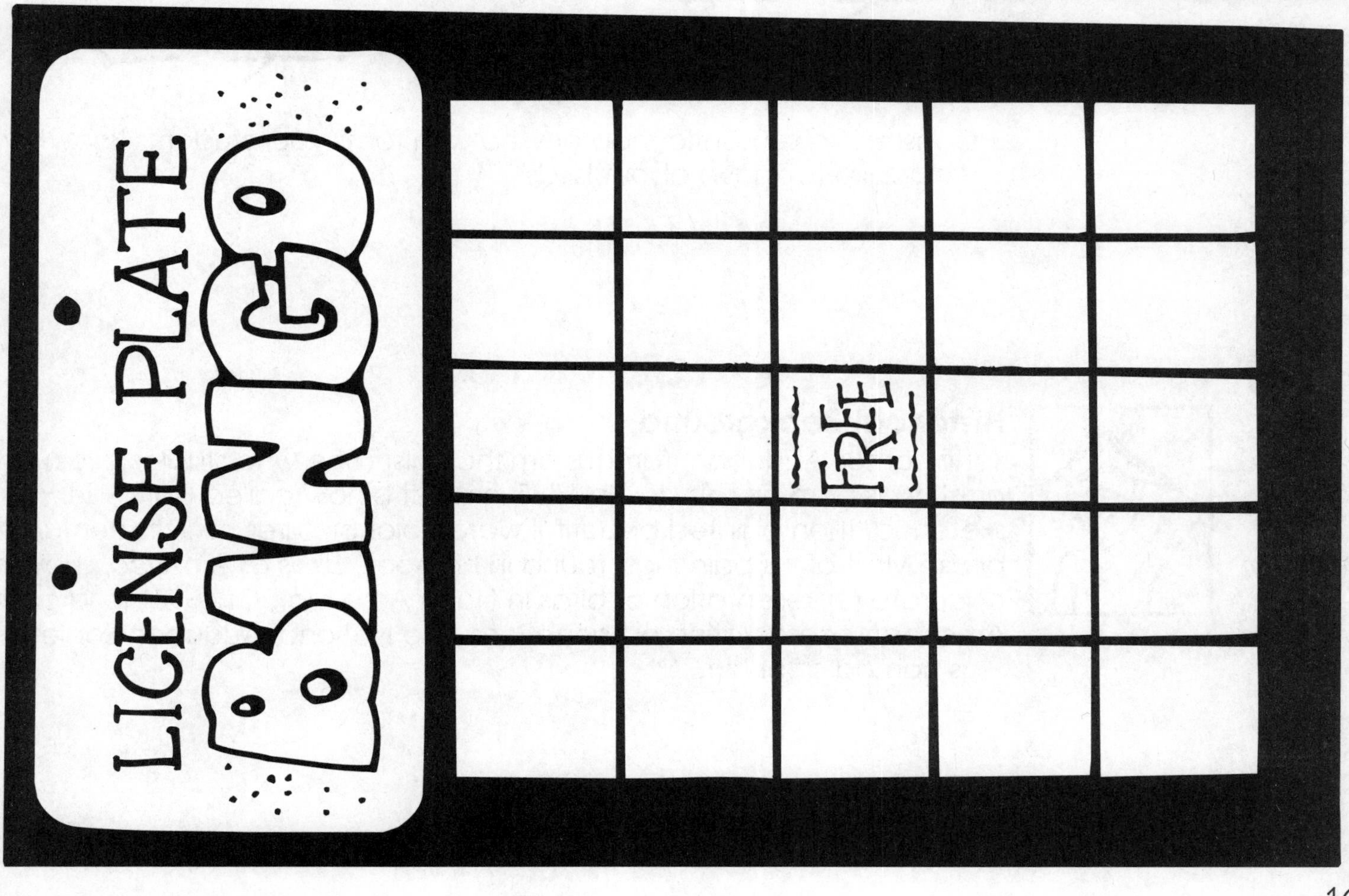
LICENSE PLATE
BINGO
FREE

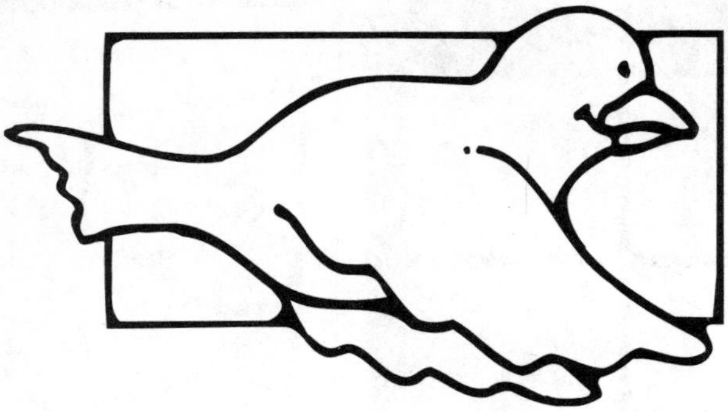

J.J. Audubon's Birthday

April 26

Setting the Stage

- Display books and pictures of birds. Ask to borrow stuffed birds, nests or other interesting items from local museums. Add them to the display. A dead branch transplanted in a pot filled with sand can be a great way to display student-made pictures of different kinds of birds.

- Make "bird tracks" with chalk or a dry-erase marker going across the front board to stimulate interest.

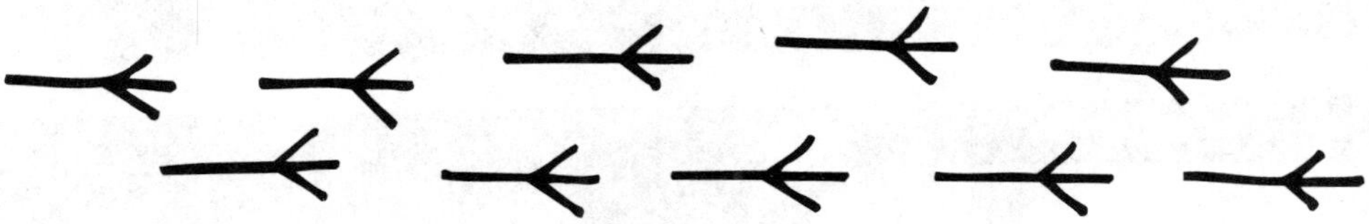

- Construct a semantic map or web with facts your students know (or would like to know) about birds.

Historical Background

John James Audubon, famous ornithologist (one who studies birds) and artist, was born on this day in 1785 in what is now called Haiti. He sketched, then painted beautiful watercolor pictures of 19th-century birds. Most of his paintings, found in his book, *Birds of America*, show an accurate representation of birds in North America. One of the largest American conservation organizations, The National Audubon Society, was named after him.

Literary Exploration

Amazing Birds by Alexandra Parsons
American Endangered Birds by Robert M. McClung
Bird by David Burnie
Bird by Moira Butterfield
The Bird Alphabet Book by Jerry Pallotta
Birds by Tessa Board
Birds by Carolyn Boulton
Birds by Jane Werner Watson
Birds by Brian Wildsmith
Birds Do the Strangest Things by Leonora and Arthur Hornblow
Birds of America by J.J. Audubon
Birds of Prey by Lynn Stone
Birds on Your Street by Seymour Simon
Capturing Nature: The Writing and Art of John James Audubon by Peter and Connie Roop
Come Again Pelican by Don Freeman
Feathers for Lunch by Lois Ehlert
Filling the Bill by Aileen Fisher
Flightless Birds by Norman Barrett
Fly, Homer Fly by Bill Peet
Have You Seen Birds? by Joanne Oppenheim
The How and Why Wonder Book of Birds by Robert Mathewson
Hummingbirds by Betty John
It's Nesting Time by Roma Gans
John Audubon: Boy Naturalist by Bobbs-Merrill
John James Audubon by Jan Gleiter
John James Audubon by Joseph Kastner
John James Audubon: Bird Artist by Garrard
John James Audubon: Artist of the Wild by Martha Kendall
A Kid's First Book of Birdwatching by Scott Weidensaul
The Kweeks of Kookatumdee by Bill Peet
The Robin Family by Frances Horwich
Robins Fly North, Robins Fly South by John Kaufman
The True Book of Birds We Know by Margaret Friskey
Trumpet of the Swan by E.B. White
What's Inside? by May Garlick
Whose Little Bird Am I? by Leonard Weisgard
A Year of Birds by Ashley Wolff

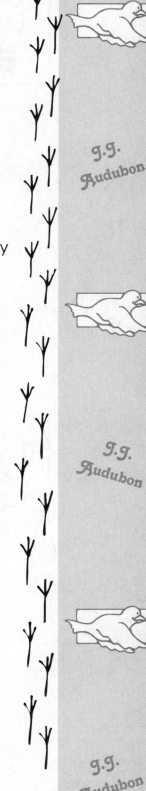

J.J. Audubon
J.J. Audubon

Language Experience

- Illustrate a Venn diagram showing the similarities and differences between a bird and a fish.

- Brainstorm together different types of birds. Print the names on the board, then let your students alphabetize them.

Writing Experience

- Let students write a "Bird's-Eye View" of a day in the life of a bird. See reproducible on page 169.

- The National Audubon Society has a wonderful supply of books, slides, pamphlets and charts about birds! Write a class letter or individual letters to:
  The National Audubon Society
  950 Third Avenue
  New York, NY 10022

Math Experience

- Let students experiment with different kinds of bird beaks. Provide plastic forks, knives and spoons, scissors, knitting needles, beads, paper clips, toothpicks and shell macaroni. Display pictures of bird beaks and have students choose matches from the items (knives—knife bill, spoons—stork bill, scissors—scissors bill, knitting needles—stabber bill. After identifying the beaks, student can take a paper cup with the remaining items (beads, paper clips, toothpicks and macaroni) and empty them on a table. Let them see how much "food" (the items on the table) they can pick up in a set time using the "beaks" they matched earlier (knives, spoons, scissors and knitting needles). Discuss which kind of beak works best with each kind of food. Graph the results on a class bar graph.

- Have students each draw a bird and a nest, then write a math problem on the nest and the answer on the bird. "Spot-check" these. Then have students trade the birds and nests with other students and try to match the problems with the correct answers. See patterns on page 170.

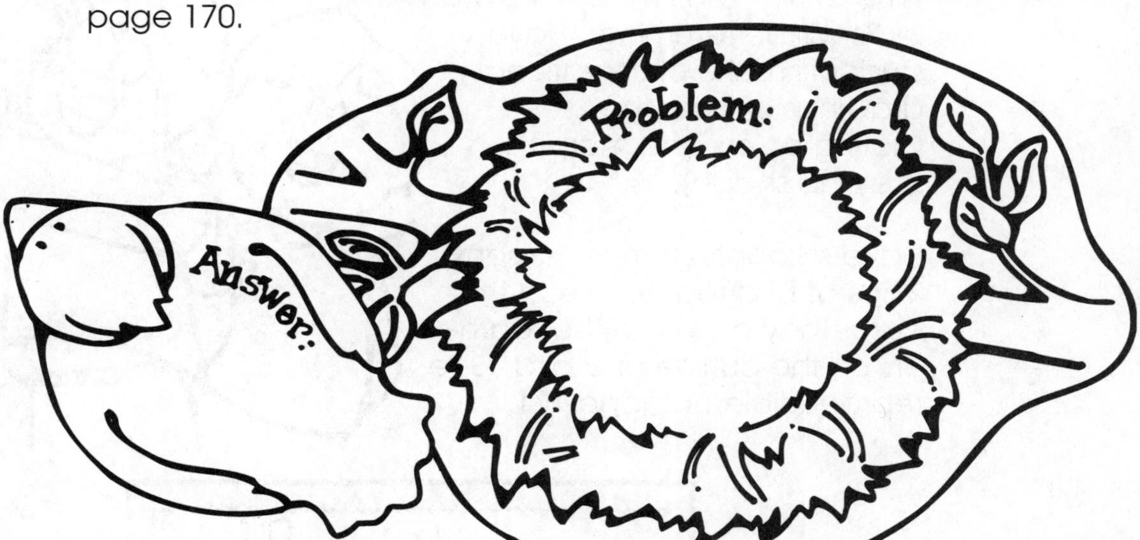

Science/Health Experience

- Begin a unit on ornithology, the study of birds.

Social Studies Experience

- Audubon painted pictures of some birds that no longer exist. Discuss endangered birds.

Music/Dramatic Experience

- Sing "Alouette," which means "pretty bird."
- Challenge students to whistle and chirp, copying specific bird calls.

Physical/Sensory Experience

- Play a game of Crows and Cranes. Divide students into two groups (Crows and Cranes). Designate a goal for each. The two groups face one another about five feet apart. Call out one of the names. The group whose name you called chases the others who are trying to get to their goal without being caught. Anyone caught becomes part of the opposite team. The winning team is the one with the most members at the end of the playing time.
- Take students on a bird watch! During this time of the year, many migratory birds will be returning. Have students make observational drawings of birds they see (noting colors and markings, size and shape).

- Have students gather as many kinds of bird feathers as they can. They can glue the feathers on the outline of a bird. See reproducible on page 171.

Arts/Crafts Experience

- Take students outside to do a little sketching and painting with watercolors, like Audubon!
- Let students make bird feeders. They can be made many ways: fill a clean, milk carton half with corn and sunflower seeds; spread peanut butter on a pinecone and top it with birdseed; fill a grapefruit half with melted suet and peanut butter; string popcorn and cranberries on heavy thread. All these feeders can be hung from a tree branch outside a window so students can watch.

- Students can make pretend binoculars from toilet paper tubes painted and glued together. Make copies of the pattern for "Flyer Spyers" on page 172.

- Have each student draw a bird and label its parts.
- Students can make an easy three-dimensional bird by gluing a smaller circle to a larger circle, then adding an eye and a beak to the small circle. They cut a slit in the center of the larger circle and fanfold a piece of paper to slip through the slit for wings.

Extension Activities

- If you're near an aviary exhibit, take your class there on a field trip!
- Have an Early Bird Breakfast. Serve whatever you like, but be sure that the "early bird gets the worm!"

⚠ Your students will love these Edible Bird Nests!

Edible Bird Nests

1 c. butterscotch chips
1/2 c. creamy peanut butter
Melt chips and mix with peanut butter.
Slowly stir in:
3 c. rice or cornflake cereal
(chow mein noodles work, too.)
Shape into bird nest shapes and leave to cool on wax paper. After nest is cool, add jelly beans or "Easter-y" speckled eggs inside the nest.

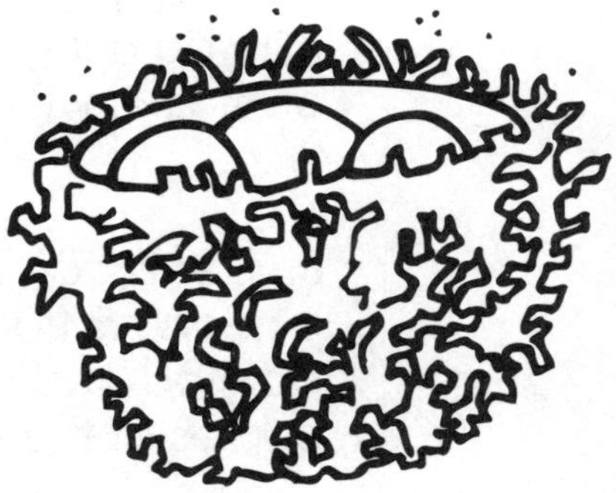

⚠ Serve this tasty treat to your students. Crush chocolate sandwich cookies to resemble dirt and put in a zip-close plastic bags with gummy worms.

- Invite a member of the local Audubon Society to visit your class to talk about birds in your area.

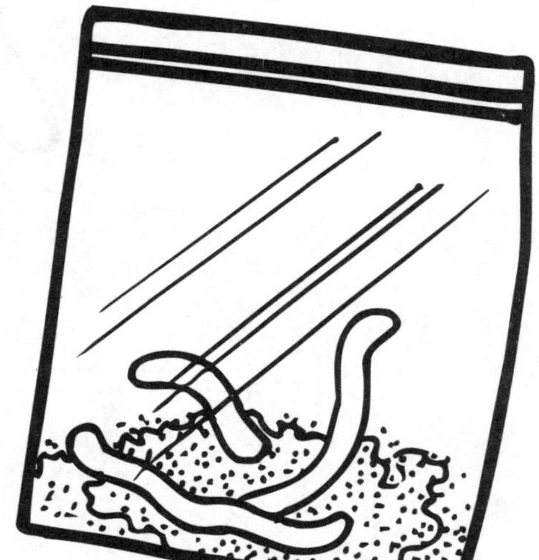

Follow-Up/Homework Idea

- Encourage students to discuss these figures of speech with their parents: "The early bird catches the worm" and "birds of a feather flock together!"

A day in the life of a...

Bird

Name:

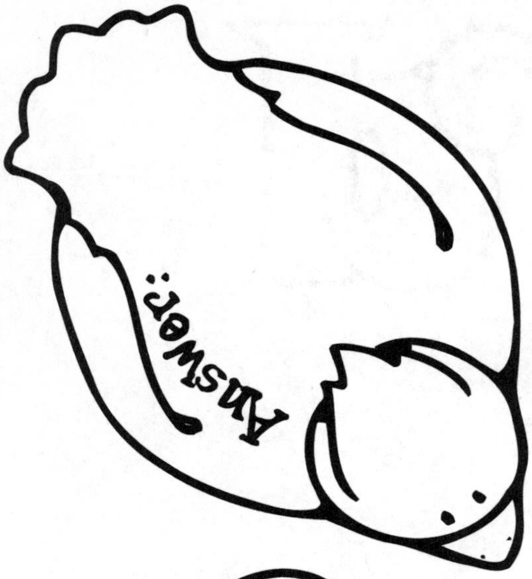
Answer:

Problem:

Problem:

Answer:

Birds of a feather

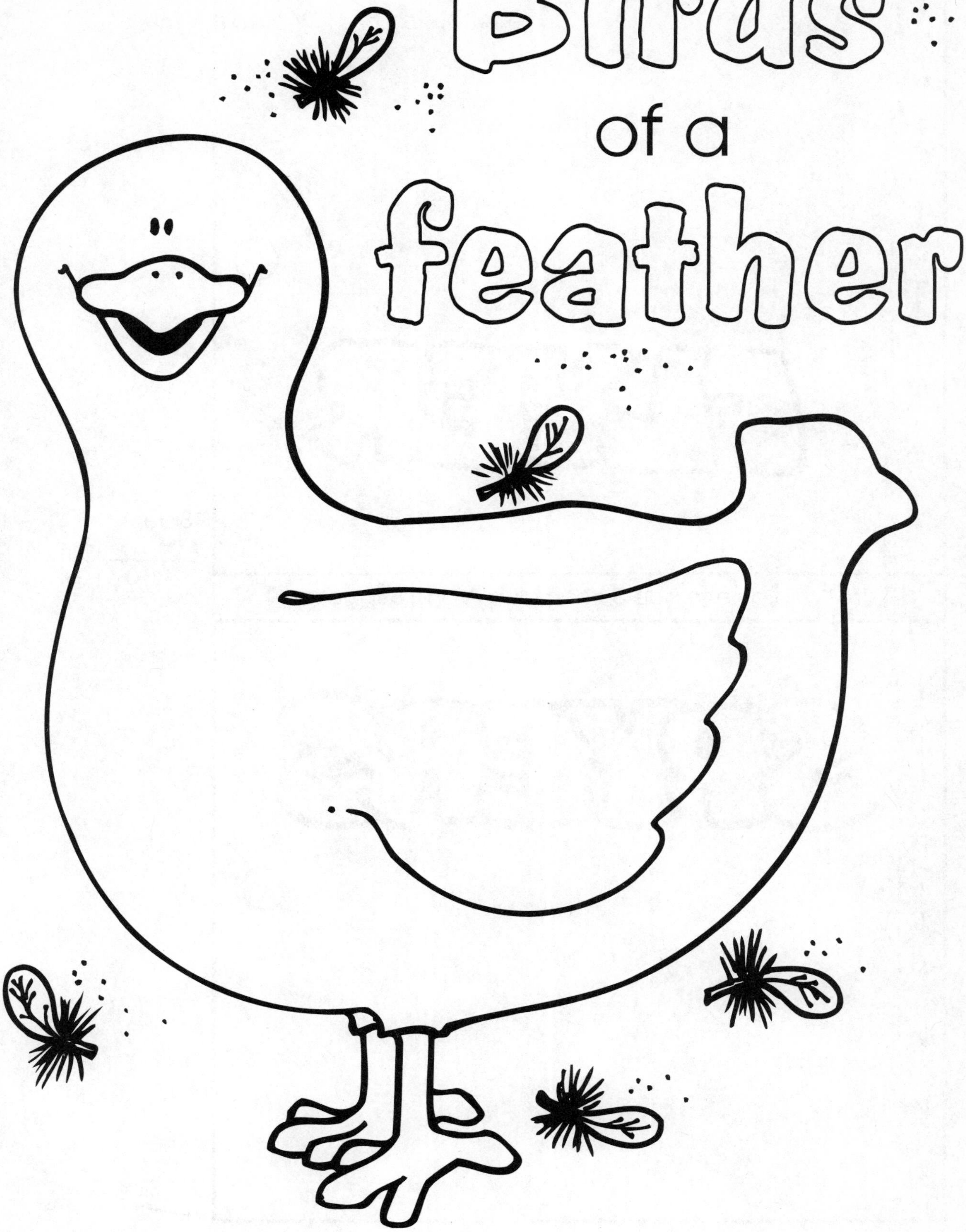

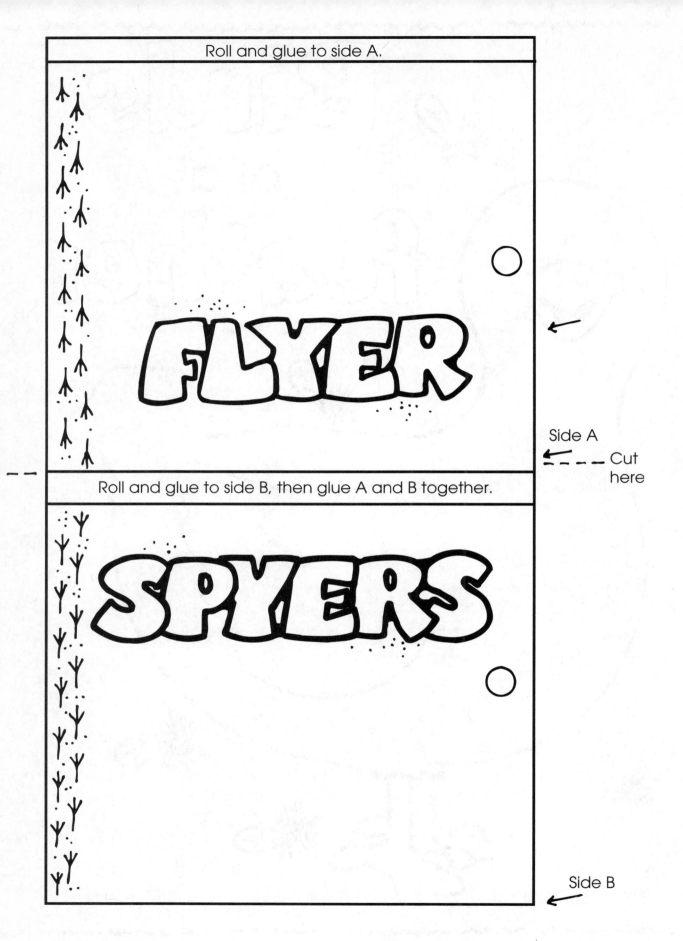

Roll and glue to side A.

FLYER

Side A

Cut here

Roll and glue to side B, then glue A and B together.

SPYERS

Side B

Pajama Party Day

April 27

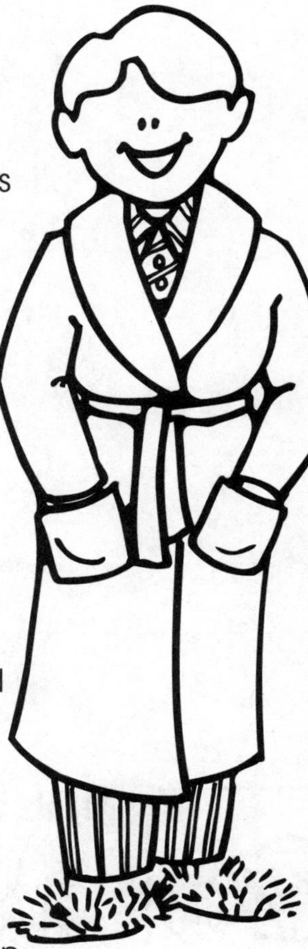

Setting the Stage

- Invite your students to come to school in pajamas today! Wear a bathrobe and house slippers to greet them.

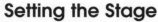

Literary Exploration

Arthur's First Sleepover by Marc Brown
Bedtime for Frances by Russell Hoban
The Cat's Pajamas by Mark Burgess
The Cat's Pajamas by Ida Chittum
I Dance in My Red Pajamas by Edith Thacher Hurd
Ira Sleeps Over by Bernard Waber
Monster Can't Sleep by Virginia Mueller
The Monster Under My Bed by Suzanne Gruber
The Monster Under My Bed by James Howe
The Napping House by Audrey Wood
Pajamas by Livingston Taylor
Porcupine's Pajama Party by Terry Webb Harshman
There's a Nightmare in My Closet by Mercer Mayer
Where the Wild Things Are by Maurice Sendak

Language Experience

- How many new words can your students make using the letters in *pajamas*?

- Challenge students to come up with adjectives to describe pajamas (comfy, cozy, warm, etc.).

Writing Experience

- Talk about nightmares. Students can describe what they do when they get scared by one. They can write on the reproducible on page176.

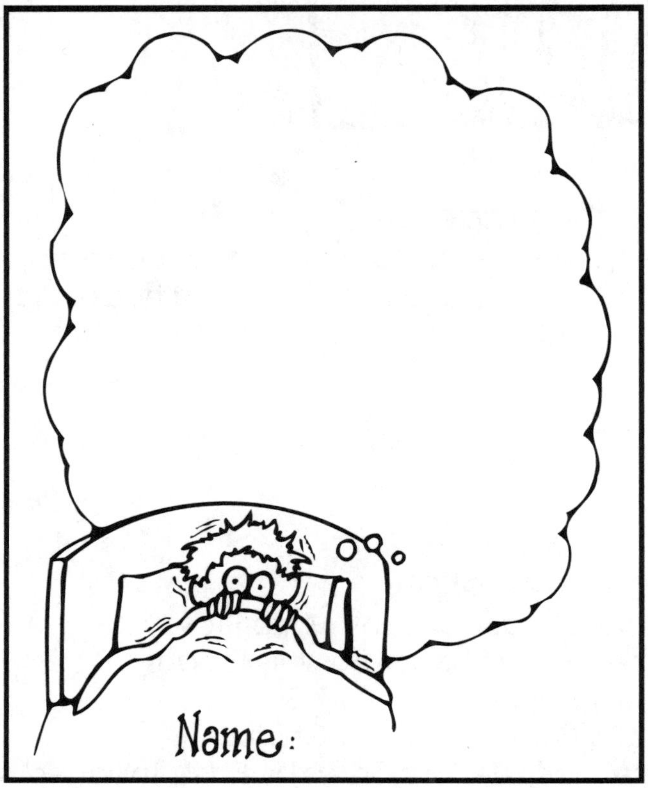

Math Experience

- Let your students survey schoolmates about their approximate amount of sleep per night. Let them show this information on a class bar graph.

Science/Health Experience

- Talk about the importance of a good night's sleep for health and well-being.

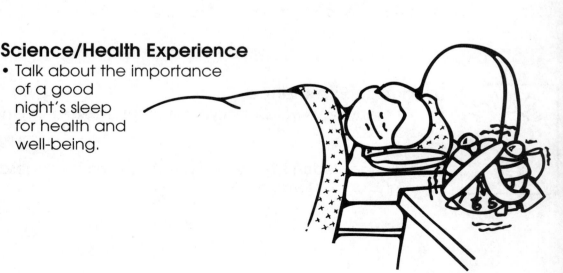

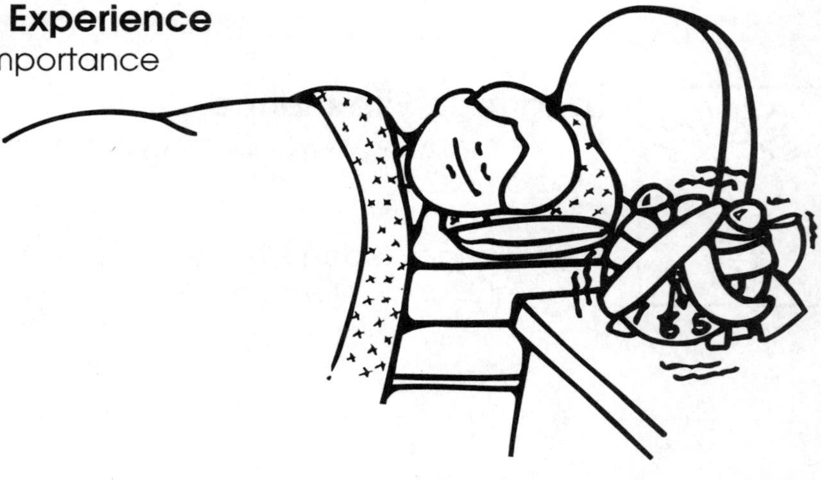

Music/Dramatic Experience

- Sing or play a tape or CD of a bedtime lullaby!
- Let students role-play how they sleep (curled up, on their backs, on their stomachs, tossing and turning, snoring, etc.).

Physical/Sensory Experience

- Younger students can enjoy a five-minute "rest period" (pajamas and all)!

Arts/Crafts Experience

- Have students draw people and animals wearing pajamas (such as llamas wearing pajamas)! What kinds of pajamas do children wear? Does a king or queen wear a crown with pajamas?

Follow-Up/Homework Idea

- Encourage students to get a good night's sleep at home tonight!

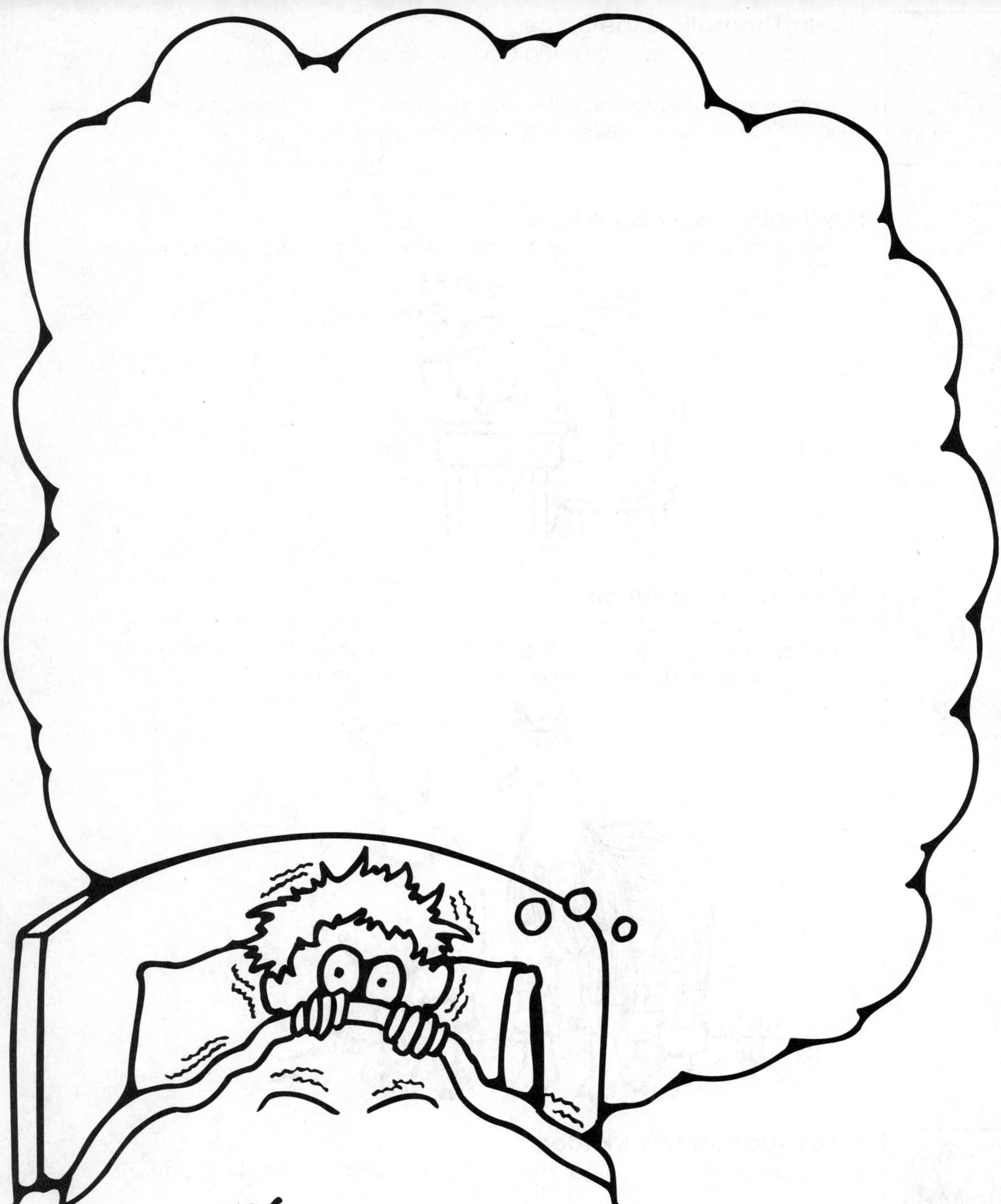

Name:

Endangered Animals Day

April 28

Setting the Stage

- Display posters and books dealing with endangered and extinct animals.

- Construct a semantic web with facts your students know about endangered animals. Then list questions they have regarding these animals.

Literary Exploration

Baby Animals: Stories of Endangered Animals by Derek Hall
Endangered Animals by Dean Morris
Endangered Animals by Malcolm Penny
Endangered Animals by Lynn Stone
Endangered Forest Animals by Dave Taylor
Endangered Grassland Animals by Dave Taylor
Endangered Mountain Animals by Dave Taylor
Endangered Wetland Animals by Dave Taylor
In Search of the Last Dodo by Ann Cartwright
MacMillan Children's Guide to Endangered Animals by Roger Few
No Dodos: A Counting Book of Endangered Animals by Amanda Wallwork
Will We Miss Them? Endangered Species by Alexandra Wright

Language Experience

- How many new words can your students make using the letters in *endangered*?
- Challenge students to think of synonyms for *endangered species*.

Writing Experience

- Ask students to imagine they are the last surviving humans or animals of their kind. Have them write about what led up to their endangered situations. See reproducible on page 180.
- Students may write about their feelings (or write letters requesting information) regarding endangered species. They can write to:

  Defenders of Wildlife
  1244 Nineteenth St., N.W.
  Washington, D.C. 20036

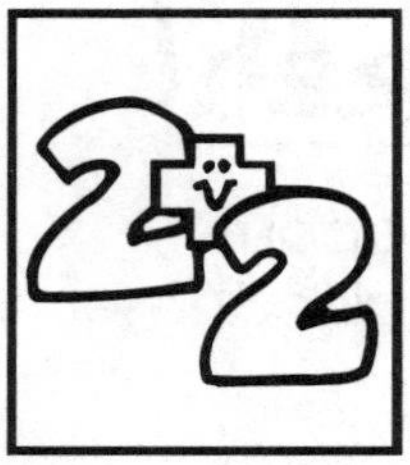

Math Experience

- Create animal story problems. (Example: There were 20 dodo birds, but 8 did not survive. How many are now endangered?) After students solve your problems, let them create their own, then exchange them and try to solve them.

Science/Health Experience

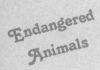

- Have students research endangered animals. Discuss what can be done to save these animals.
- Discuss how animals become endangered.

Social Studies Experience

- Students can research areas of the world that are in danger of losing their habitat (rain forest, tundra, wetlands). Have them locate the areas on a world map.

Physical/Sensory Experience

- Play "jungle" music as students play Don't Become Extinct Musical Chairs. Each student is given the name of an endangered animal while he or she is playing. When someone is eliminated from the game for not having a chair, that "animal" becomes extinct.

Arts/Crafts Experience

- Let students create posters about saving endangered animals. Get permission to hang these around the school and in your community to increase public awareness about the plight of these animals.

- Students can work together to create a giant mural of endangered animals throughout the world.

Extension Activities

- Invite a member or representative of the Wildlife Association to come and speak to your class about what they can do to help endangered animals everywhere.

Follow-Up/Homework Idea

- Encourage your students to be careful not to disturb any animal, bird or insect habitats on the way home or in their neighborhoods.

YOU ARE THE LAST...

Giant Fun Day

April 29

Setting the Stage

- Put down giant footprints leading into the classroom. Create a beanstalk of twisted green crepe paper up to the ceiling. Place miniature items around the classroom so students can see what it would feel like to be a giant. See patterns on pages 186-187. (Enlarge the patterns to 11" x 17" for giant footprints!)

- Construct a semantic web with words your students think of when you say the word *giant*.

Historical Background

Since the days of David and Goliath, people have been fascinated by giants. They were important characters in many of the earliest fables and fairy tales and continue to be a popular feature in children's literature.

Literary Exploration

BFG (Big Friendly Giant) by Roald Dahl
Big Jeremy by Steven Kroll
The Biggest Boy by Kevin Henkes
David and the Giant by Emily Little
Donkey, Nina and the Giant by John Carroll
The Dwarf Giant by Anita Lobel
Enormous Crocodile by Roald Dahl
Giant Animals by H.E. Smith
The Giant Fish and Other Stories by Otto Svend
Giant John by Arnold Lobel
The Giant's Toe by Brock Cole
Giant Water Bugs by Kathleen Pohl
Giant Work Machine by Thea Feldman
The Great Quillow by James Thurber
Gulliver's Adventures in Lilliput by Jonathan Swift
Gustav, the Gourmet Giant by LouAnn Biggs Gaeddert
Harry Hoyle's Giant Jumping Bean by William Van Horn
In Search of the Giant by Jeanne Willis
Jack, the Giant Chaser by Kenn Compton
James and the Giant Peach by Roald Dahl
Jim and the Beanstalk by Raymond Briggs
Learning About Giants by Ruth Shannon Odor
Little Hen and the Giant by Maria Polushkin
Little Wolf and the Giant by Sue Porter
My Backyard Giant by Mary Sawicki
Paul Bunyan by Steven Kellogg
Rude Giants by Audrey Wood
The Selfish Giant by Oscar Wilde
Shhh! by Sally Grindley
What Can a Giant Do? by Mary Louise Cuneo

Language Experience

- Let students brainstorm synonyms for the word *giant* (*huge, large, big, humongous, enormous, gigantic,* etc.). Then have them think of antonyms (*tiny, teeny, little, small,* etc.).

Writing Experience

- Students can write stories using these story starters:
  I would like a great BIG . . .
  If I were a giant, I would . . .
  I couldn't believe it, but right before my very eyes was the biggest . . .
  See reproducible on page 188.

Math Experience

- After reading from the *BFG (Big Friendly Giant)* or other giant story, let students draw a giant on a large sheet of butcher paper, then measure it. Ask them how tall they think a real giant might be. Students can paint the giant later in the day.

- Make up some math problems with "giant" numbers.
  (Example: 5280 - 1240 = ?)

Social Studies Experience

- Learn about giants from other cultures! Read *The Mysterious Giant of Barletta: An Italian Folktale* by Tomie de Paola, *Abiyoyo: Based on a South African Lullaby & Folk Song* by Pete Seeger or *The Hungry Giant of the Tundra* written by Teri Sloat.

- Ask students to suggest other "giant" things (mountains, animals, buildings, etc.).

Music/Dramatic Experience

- Let students role-play walking as a giant might walk as you play a tape or CD of big-band music.

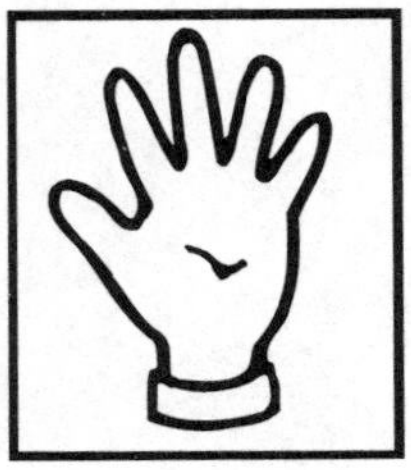

Physical/Sensory Experience

- Play Fee-Fi-Fo-Fum (like Duck, Duck, Goose). One student walks around a circle of students, tapping shoulders saying, "Fee-Fi-Fo-Fum." When the student taps someone on the shoulder and says, "Jack," the tapped student runs around the circle and tries to get back to his place before the tapper does.

- Play Sleeping Giant. One player is chosen to be the giant who must protect his "treasures" (small objects). He closes his eyes and "sleeps" on a chair while the others try to take his "treasures." If he catches them, the giant puts them in the dinner pot (another chair). If the students taking the treasure "freeze," the giant thinks they are statues, but if they move, he can catch them. Play until everyone gets caught.

Arts/Crafts Experience

- Stock up on a lot of white butcher paper for this project! Students decide upon an object (pencil, shoe, etc.) that they want to paint and then they create it by magnifying it about 10 times. In other words, GIANT art! Display these all over the walls or hall.

Extension Activities

⚠ Make GIANT cookies. Buy refrigerator cookie dough and let students shape their own huge cookies. For sanitary purposes, each student can "wear" a sandwich bag on each hand as they shape the cookie. Bake the cookies according to directions. Let students decorate them, then take GIANT bites!

Values Education Experience

- Some people dream of "making it BIG" someday. Discuss what that means. Ask students what *success* means to them. How can they "make it big" and be successful right now?

Follow-Up/Homework Idea

- Challenge students to take giant steps on the way home or around their neighborhoods.

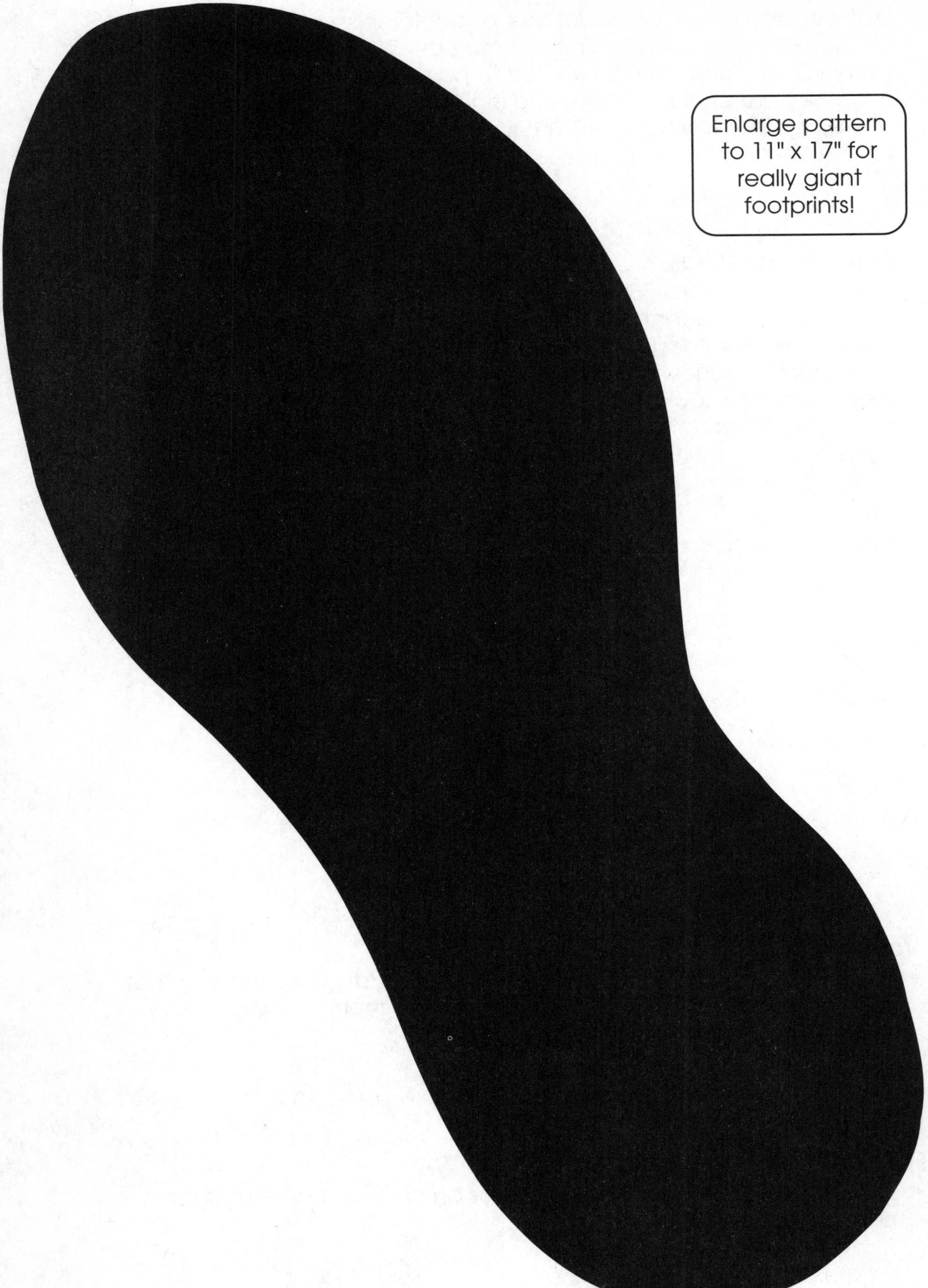

Enlarge pattern to 11" x 17" for really giant footprints!

Louisiana Statehood Day

April 30

Setting the Stage

- Display posters from a travel agency and literature about Louisiana to gather excitement and interest in today's activities.

Historical Background

Louisiana became a state on this day in 1812, the 18th state in the Union. It's known as the Pelican State. In fact, the state flag shows a pelican on its nest. Louisiana has a rich history, first claimed by the French, named after King Louis XIV.

Literary Exploration

Louisiana by Kathleen Thompson
Louisiana in Words and Pictures by Dennis B. Fradin
The Story of the Louisiana Purchase by Mary Kay Phelan

Language Experience

- Create a Venn diagram depicting the similarities and differences between a Louisiana bayou alligator and a crocodile.

- Study some of the speech dialects used in Louisiana such as Cajun.

Science/Health Experience

- Learn about crocodiles and alligators and their habitats in the Louisiana bayou.

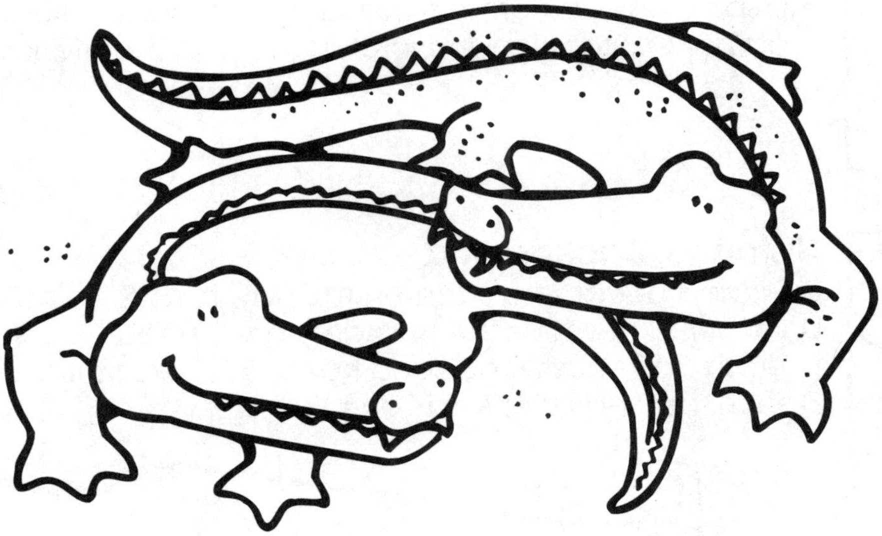

Louisiana Statehood

Social Studies Experience

- Research the state of Louisiana and find out what makes Louisiana unique.

- Find out about the city of New Orleans, Louisiana. How was it affected by Hurricane Katrina in the summer of 2005? How old is this historic city? For what is it famous?

Louisiana Statehood

Music/Dramatic Experience

- Borrow New Orleans jazz music from a local library and play it quietly in the background as students work.

Physical/Sensory Experience

- Let students dance to Louisiana jazz. They can make up their own dances.

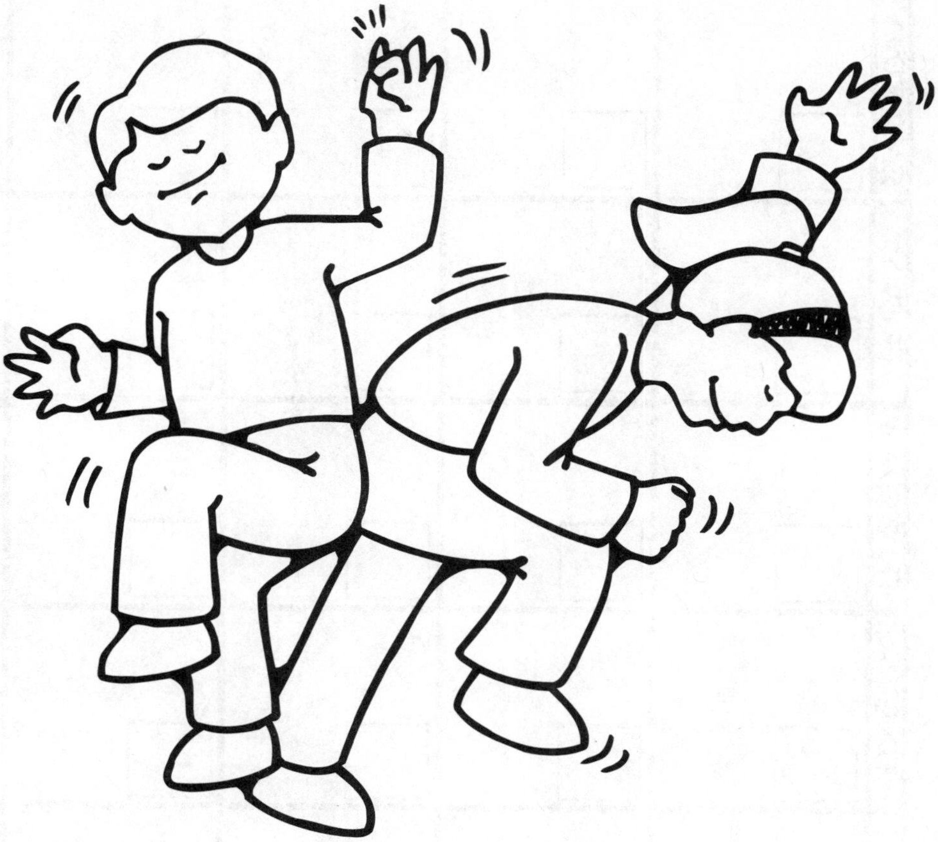

Arts/Crafts Experience

- Students can create Louisiana state flags or salt dough relief maps.
- Have students work together to create a Louisiana bayou mural, including flowers, trees and animals that can be found there.
- Challenge students to create Mardi Gras masks and costumes.

Extension Activities

⚠ Celebrate New Orleans Mardi Gras! Hold a carnival with students wearing masks and colorful costumes they have made. They can throw confetti (hole-punched paper circles), blow noisemakers and dance to New Orleans music. Serve Cajun or spicy hot wings for a special treat.

APRIL

SUNDAY	MONDAY	TUESDAY	WEDNESDAY	THURSDAY	FRIDAY	SATURDAY

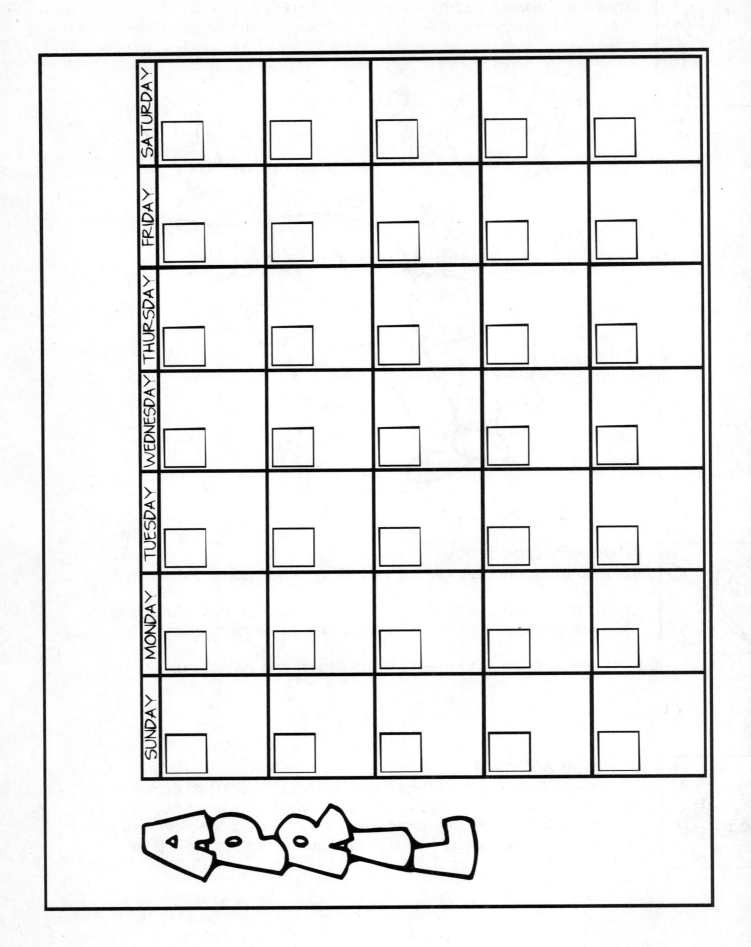